ONE HUNDRED FILMS AND A FUNERAL

DOODLE OF MICHAEL KUHN BY ROBERT REDFORD

ONE HUNDRED FILMS
AND A
FUNERAL

Michael Kuhn

Re-printed by Thorogood 2003

10-12 Rivington Street London EC2A 3DU

Telephone: 020 7749 4748

Fax: 020 7729 6110

Email: info@thorogood.ws

A CIP catalogue record for this book is available from
the British Library.

ISBN 1 85418 216 1

Cover and Book designed by Driftdesign.

Printed in India by Replika Press Pvt. Ltd.

PolyGram Filmed Entertainment – I can't help think of somebody in their teens who got shot in the back. That's probably what it will be remembered for. A child who was growing remarkably well and got shot in the back …and died.

ALAIN LÉVY, FORMERLY PRESIDENT AND CEO, POLYGRAM NV

Dedication

In loving memory of George Kuhn 1907-1978

Contents

PART TWO
Influences, titans and characters

PART THREE
Some other bit-parts observed

Illustrations

Preface

The end, as is often the case, couldn't have been more mundane. In mid 1998, I was sitting in my top floor conference room at PolyGram's London offices in St. James Square ('toney St. James Square' as *Variety* would say). My assistant told me that my boss, Alain Lévy, wished to see me in the boardroom. As I had done hundreds of times before, I climbed the two flights of stairs to the very modern but rather anonymous board-room on the fourth floor, where I found Alain smiling nervously and chain smoking.

'Guess What?' he said.

I gave him the pause he was looking for and then he continued 'The buggers have sold us'. By 'buggers' he meant Philips, one of Holland's largest companies. Philips owned approximately 75 per cent of PolyGram and had been selling light bulbs and other stuff for the last 100 years from their base in Eindhoven in the Netherlands. More about them in due course.

It was pretty clear that things were bad. When a company owns another company with such a large shareholding and decides to sell it, there's generally no way to stop them. And so began futile, but strenuous efforts on behalf of the management of PolyGram, myself and Alain Lévy included, to try to save PolyGram from annihilation. Rather predictably, this effort failed and what had been a wonderful European company is now no more – perhaps only existing in the memory of those people who spent their careers building it up and creating fabulous values for their shareholders.

This story does not concentrate so much on the greater part of the PolyGram story – the wonderful collection of assets that at one time comprised music publishing catalogues such as Chappell, classical music catalogues such as Deutsche Grammophon and Philips, pop catalogues such as Polydor, Mercury, Island Records, A&M and jazz catalogues like Verve. Rather, this is the story of PolyGram Filmed Entertainment, which began operations in January 1992 and effectively shut down at the end of 1998.

In the few moments it took to digest Alain's news, a realisation dawned that this would be the end of PolyGram Filmed Entertainment. Although it might have been anticipated that our seeming ally – our principal share-holder Philips – was the greatest enemy, it is certainly something that I would never have believed. I had assumed that if PolyGram Films failed it would be my fault, the failure of our movies, the failure of the plan that we had laid at the beginning of 1991, or a lack of commitment by my colleagues on the board of PolyGram. I would not have thought that the enemy within, our Dutch masters, would have been the instrument by which we were executed.

So this is the story of building a film studio from scratch. More than that, it is the story of the first attempts to build a world-wide Hollywood style film business based in Europe.

Telling the story, it is inevitable that one will touch on some of the great characters that have influenced me and continue so to do, and that one will draw out some of the lessons learned in this great enterprise. Unlike, however, an old general in a gentleman's club in London replaying old battles using the table cutlery, this exercise hopefully will be a prelude to a new attempt to do (this time successfully) what was not quite accom-plished with PolyGram Films.

While any book such as this is bound to be self-regarding, I have in mind how helpful it would have been had the exemplar of building a studio from scratch, someone who influenced my thinking in every-thing I did at PolyGram Films, been able to commit to writing his own story of the building up of what must have been the greatest post-war studio in America, United Artists – the great figure of Arthur Krim. Had I had the benefit of knowing him, if not in person, at least through a book such as this, it would have eased the way considerably.

Michael Kuhn April 2002, London

Acknowledgements

I would like to acknowledge the invaluable assistance of David Sorfa who conducted much of the research and undertook interviews for me; to my assistant Alexandra Arlango; to Neil Thomas for his ideas on structure; to many former colleagues including Alain Lévy, Tim Bevan, Jane Moore, Wolfgang Hix, Claudia Gray, Gary Shoefield, Steve Golin, Wendy Palmer, Stewart Till, Jill Tandy, Malcolm Richie and most particularly Richard Constant. I have tried to acknowledge other sources in the text. Errors, as they say, are mine and will hopefully be indulged.

Michael Kuhn

"…it (PolyGram Filmed Entertainment) probably came closer, with the exception of DreamWorks, than anybody else who has come to create a studio in the last 40 or 50 years… There was a proper strategic vision to it. "

TIM BEVAN, CO-PRESIDENT, WORKING TITLE

PART ONE

PolyGram and films – the ins and outs

1
Early flirtations

PolyGram's first flings

At its height, PolyGram was the biggest music company in the world with music operations in 42 countries, revenues in excess of US$6 billion and an implied value to shareholders of US$10 billion.

The origins of this company were so characteristic of the slow and rather archaic growth of multi-nationals based in Europe, that they are worth recalling.

In the very early 1960s, among the old guard Titans of European owner/managers, two figures stood out above the rest. Frits Philips of the Dutch Philips Group and Ernst von Siemens, of Siemens Group in Germany were figures of world-renown in the business community. Each of them had a small but similar problem in that both groups owned small music companies which had not much to do with their core business. Philips owned Deutsche Grammophon and Siemens owned Philips Records.

The two Presidents agreed to merge their entertainment activities with effect from 1st October 1962. For tax reasons, it was decided, rather than to set up one holding company, to have a joint venture with equal and distinct head offices, one in Hamburg, West Germany and the other in Baarn in the Netherlands. To begin with they didn't even have a common name – the name PolyGram not coming into being until 1972. The joint venture went under the extraordinary acronym 'GPG', which everyone at Philips called 'Group Philips Grammophon' while their German colleagues preferred to call it 'Grammophon Philips Groupen'.

Although the name was unwieldy, the operations of the two companies fitted neatly together. Philips had been strong in the Netherlands, but with such a small home base, it had to look to the other territories in order to gain size and as a consequence was relatively strong internationally. Deutsche Grammophon, on the other hand, was extremely strong in the very large and profitable territories of Germany, Austria and German speaking Switzerland but was very weak internationally.

At the management level the traditional and rather rigid management style inherited from Siemens matched quite well with the more lax but English speaking international style of the Philips management. Siemens lacked a consumer touch, given that their customer base was principally in heavy industry, whereas a large part of Philips' business had to do with the normal retail consumer of their electronics products.

The merger of the two entities, however, was not in itself a guarantee of success. Perhaps of more interest was that in 1963 the Beatles topped the UK charts for the first time with their second single *Please Please Me*. From then on the modern record industry happened with a vengeance and the PolyGram joint venture benefited from the tremendous growth in revenues and profitability of the record business.

One of the greatest acquisitions during that period, was of the wonderful music publishing company, Chappell Music. This was acquired in 1967 for US$42.5 million (and its subsequent sale in the mid 80s for in excess of US$100 million saved PolyGram at a time of penury).

The uneasy legal structure tainted by tax needs had, however, failed to produce a management structure capable of riding the turbulent growth that had overtaken PolyGram through the 1970s. Things came to a head at the end of the decade.

In 1977 PolyGram released the sound track to the movie *Saturday Night Fever* and in 1978 the sound track to *Grease*. Each of these sound tracks shipped in excess of 20 million units, but the important word to note is 'shipped'. In the United States, where a large percentage of the shipments were made, business was done on a 'sale or return' basis. So while apparent prosperity on an unprecedented scale showed up in PolyGram's books in 1978 and 1979, by 1980 and 1981 returns of unsold shipments began to have a negative impact on the results of the company. This might have been less of a problem had it not been for the fact that, at the same time, one of the worst recessions ever experienced in the music business had taken hold on a world-wide basis. Furthermore, an ill-advised move into feature film production in Hollywood had led to financial disaster.

The lack of a cohesive management, insufficient infrastructure to track and deal with the problem of returns of records from retailers and the large losses in the film operations combined to produce a crisis.

As 1979 turned into 1980, another problem loomed. 1982 was the end of the 20 year joint venture between Philips and Siemens. While the partnership remained, PolyGram's results were not consolidated on either the books of Philips or of Siemens. However, should one party buy out the other party's interests, it would also have to take all results (positive or negative) on to its books. Neither was keen to do this. For Siemens there was no reason whatsoever to buy out Philips. For Philips, however, there was an important need to retain PolyGram's significant music catalogues since Philips, together with Sony of Japan, were about to launch the compact disc and needed PolyGram's catalogues for that purpose.

Most of the management of PolyGram, who had been in place since its beginnings in 1962, left at the end of 1981 and, after an interim period of two years, capably presided over by Dr Wolfgang Hix, Philips appointed their Head of Operations in South Africa, Jan Timmer, to take over at PolyGram. Timmer spent his first three years trying to find a joint venture partner to replace Siemens in PolyGram – without success.

He also successfully launched CD Audio as a system and the introduction of CD as a replacement for black vinyl discs revolutionised the fortunes of the music business, which was to enter a new period of prosperity. Jan Timmer's ability to convince Philips not to shut down PolyGram but to retain it without a partner, instituted the last very successful period of the PolyGram story. After an earlier abortive attempt to have a public offering of 20 per cent of PolyGram's shares, it was eventually floated in 1989 at US$ 16.5 (NLG 31.5) a share. It's interesting to note that immediately prior to the sale of PolyGram to Seagram in 1998, the shares were at US$ 60.5 (NLG 115).

Jan Timmer's ability to save PolyGram from being sold or shut down and save the record industry by the introduction of CD, was only possible because he had a very able second lieutenant in the shape of David Fine, a fellow business man from South Africa, whom had been brought in initially to run the UK business and subsequently to serve as President of PolyGram in the late 1980s.

JAN TIMMER

Timmer talent-spotted Alain Lévy, an executive at CBS (initially CBS International and then CBS France). He brought him in to run PolyGram France and turn it from a loss making entity into the jewel of PolyGram's crown. He then nominated him his successor and it was Alain Lévy who led the company until its sale in 1998. During that period the shareholder value of PolyGram grew from US$ 2.8 billion to US$ 10.4 billion (the price for which it was sold to Seagram).

The new regime under Alain Lévy was the one I joined to start PolyGram Films. It was clear to this new generation of management of PolyGram, that the CD boom could not last forever; eventually everybody would have a CD player and would have replaced their black vinyl catalogue and the music business would plateau. However, shareholders had grown used to a double-digit growth in revenues and profits and would not be satisfied with any less. Where was that continued growth to come from? The internet was not even a glint in the eye of Bill Gates. The massive consolidations of the film, television and music industries that were to happen in the latter part of the 1990s had not yet occurred.

The business of PolyGram was entertainment content. We began to explore the possibility of either buying or building a filmed entertainment division. We went into it with our eyes open, knowing that it would require a massive amount of capital and a long-term commitment. It was judged that the cash flow from the music operations was so substantial and the management at PolyGram so sound in combining creative licence and financial discipline, that there was a reasonable chance of success, provided it was embarked upon in a careful and step-by-step manner. So, with the approval of my plan by the boards of PolyGram and Philips in the latter part of 1991, I began the odyssey of PolyGram Filmed Entertainment.

Before we get to that point (taken up in Chapter 4), it is interesting to look at PolyGram's various flirtations with the film business.

PolyGram's first disastrous entry into film

Wolfgang Hix was President of PolyGram for one year in 1983. Before that he was General Counsel for PolyGram and was with the company for most of its history from its very earliest years. He started his professional career at UFA (Universum Film AG), one of the greatest names in German motion picture history. From his experience at UFA he knew in an era that pre-dated home video and pay television, that the film business was extremely risky. However, in the mid 1970s when PolyGram seemed to be growing strongly and had considerable cash flows, the management began to consider expansion into filmed entertainment. There seemed some superficial synergies – soundtracks were a very big business and soundtracks came from movies. There seemed to be some cross over between music artists and film acting and, perhaps most importantly, some of the important producers were common to both the film business and the music business.

Nonetheless, to begin with, PolyGram was extremely cautious and the engagement with film came about almost by accident. In the mid 1970s PolyGram was introduced to a very successful record producer, Neil Bogart and his partner Peter Guber. The two were related by marriage. Peter Guber having worked in Hollywood, had set up as an independent and produced the hit movie *The Deep*. Bogart had managed the successful independent record company Budda Records and had recently signed Donna Summer. Charmed by Bogart and fired by the need to ally with American producer talent, PolyGram bought into Casablanca Record and Filmworks in 1977 (a company created by merging Bogart's Casablanca Records with Peter Guber's Film Company).

According to Nancy Griffin and Kim Masters' book on John Peters and Peter Guber, *Hit and Run*, it was estimated that PolyGram paid between US$10 million and US$15 million for a half share in Casablanca Records and Filmworks. Having just acquired the United Artists music distribution system, it was necessary to 'fill up the pipeline' and the product of the joint venture company would be a useful addition. Despite incredible corporate profligacy at Casablanca, the company flourished and a plethora of successful disco records in the late 1970s made it increasingly hard to control the company. Two movies made by Casablanca but not financed by PolyGram (*Thank God, It's Friday* (Robert Klane, 1978) and *Midnight Express* (Alan Parker, 1978)) had successful soundtrack albums, Donna Summer was huge and Casablanca was a hot bed of disco records. To this day, The Village People remain emblematic of an era of theatrical hedonism and popular success. Never afraid of diversity, Casablanca signed acts such as *Kiss* in addition to disco.

The end of the 1970s and the beginning of the 80s saw several interesting developments: as PolyGram fought to get control of Casablanca, Guber persuaded them to back him in setting up a fully fledged film studio called PolyGram Pictures. Quite separately, a terminally ill Bogart was eased out of the company and Guber teamed up with his long-term friend and business partner, John Peters. The venture was ill thought out as PolyGram sought to control two of the most mercurial talents in Hollywood, through the affable but quite unsuited figure of Eckhart Haas, a German TV executive who had worked for PolyGram for some years. In addition, a seasoned film executive, Gordon Stulberg, had been hired to bring some sense to the organisation, but it was difficult, if not impossible, for anyone to control Guber and Peters.

Lessons from disaster

As I looked back on this episode some years later, several interesting aspects of what was to turn into a significant financial disaster struck me:

- Even people with a record of success in the movie business were not guaranteed success by volume production.

  PolyGram Pictures made *King of the Mountain* (Noel Nosseck, 1981), *Endless Love* (Franco Zeffirelli, 1981), *Deadly Blessing* (Wes Craven, 1981), *An American Werewolf in London* (John Landis, 1981), *Six Weeks* (Tony Bill, 1982), *Split Image* (Ed Otcheff,1982) and *Pursuit of D.B. Cooper* (Roger Spottiswoode, 1982). Even though *Werewolf* was a successful film, the structure of the business was such that the main beneficiary was the director, John Landis.

- One couldn't control a Hollywood entity from Europe.

- The film business would only make financial sense if one produced a sufficiently large portfolio of movies. Five movies were unlikely to be enough. However, one of the movies developed by PolyGram Pictures was *Batman* and had that been produced by PolyGram, it might well have been that the total slate would have been a success.

- PolyGram Pictures did not have its own US distribution (it distributed its pictures through a deal with Universal Studios), nor did it have international world-wide distribution. Inability to capture the world-wide profits of the slate of movies and inability to market the movies on a world-wide basis was a fatal flaw in the plan.

- It was certainly unwise to award executives or producers excessively for getting movies into production: volume rather than quality would inevitably result.

The movie business had changed significantly since the beginning of the 1980s in that two very significant revenue sources had developed in the meantime; pay television and home video. When PolyGram Pictures was at its height, if a movie failed at the box office (as the majority of PolyGram Pictures' movies had) there was little fall back.

As it was, by the end of 1981, PolyGram had had enough, threw in the towel and Guber and Peters left the film company. The episode cost PolyGram some US$100 million (at the time) and important assets were either undersold – for example the very big film *Flash Dance* (Adrian Lyne, 1983) was sold as a development property for a paltry sum to Paramount, while Guber and Peters took *Batman* to Warners, leaving PolyGram Pictures with only a small royalty. Fortuitously the sound track album for *Flash Dance* remained with PolyGram Records and was a huge hit in 1983.

As a result of this first disastrous foray into film, the film business was considered forbidden territory within PolyGram for most of the 1980s and I used to joke that even record sleeves were suspect because of their visual content.

Robert Stigwood

Before moving off the ancient history of the group, there is one other character that needs an introduction: Robert Stigwood. Born in Australia, he had at one point set out to become a priest but after a spell as a copywriter for an Adelaide advertising agent, he left for London in 1955 and became an independent record producer. He worked for

ROBERT STIGWOOD

Courtesy RGA

Brian Epstein, the manager of the Beatles and by the mid 1960s had joined Epstein as co-manager of his company NEMS (originally the North End Road Music Stores), which had record rights to the Cream and the BeeGees. Stigwood also had an option to buy shares in NEMS. In the mid 1960s PolyGram began negotiating to buy NEMS – a process that was ended with Epstein's death on the 27 August 1967. In this way

PolyGram came to know Robert Stigwood and agreed to finance him in a new venture – The Robert Stigwood Organisation (RSO). In addition to launching the BeeGees' career, promoting Cream and other successful artists such as Eric Clapton, he backed Andrew Lloyd-Webber and Tim Rice in their productions of *Hair* and *Jesus Christ Superstar*.

Halved by Polygram, RSO went public in the late 1960s, but almost immediately discovered that the volatile nature of the record business does not fit easily with the obligations of a public company and the flotation was very unsuccessful. Stigwood soon found he had no taste for running a public company. In due course this led to a delisting and Stigwood leaving for the United States of America. In 1977 Stigwood produced *Saturday Night Fever* (John Badham) and in 1978, *Grease* (Randal Kleiser). The sound track albums for these two films were distributed by PolyGram and shipped out a staggering total in excess of 40 million copies world-wide, generating hundreds of millions of dollars in revenue and tens of millions in profit. Unfortunately, the charismatic Stigwood became very difficult for PolyGram management to control and understand.

Putting together the Casablanca story with that of Stigwood and adding in the establishment of PolyGram Pictures, results in a tale of extraordinary highs and lows. This obscure European joint venture called PolyGram had grown like Topsy on the back of the success of the music business. Led by a Philips nominee, Coen Solleveld, who managed to keep a Dutch/German joint venture strong, it had become a significant world-wide operation. At the end of the 1970s, it was enjoying the fruits of two of the biggest hit albums ever seen in pop history. At the same time, buoyed by an unjustified confidence in their future success, the management gambled in the film business and lost heavily.

But the bad news had only just begun. A world recession started in the music industry; in large markets such as the United States, where records were sold on a 'sale or return' basis, returns exceeded sales; the market leader, CBS records, responded by price cutting, which other companies had to follow and the result was a reduction of profits in the record business to an extent never before experienced. PolyGram, with its less developed infrastructure, suffered more than many and new management, new visions, new disciplines were called for. It was about this time that I stopped being a record company lawyer and took my first faltering steps on the executive ladder.

2
When a film is not a film: the long form music video disguise

PolyGram Pictures and PolyGram Music Video

Born in Africa, I came back to school in England in 1962 and after attending Clare College, Cambridge, qualified as an English lawyer in 1972. After a short spell at the leading London law firm of Denton Hall & Burgin, I joined PolyGram and, with a short break, was there from 1975 until I left in 1998.

The bit of PolyGram I joined in the early 1970s was Polydor Records. Those were the days when the music business was more fun than business. Few of the executives could have told the difference between a profit and loss account and a balance sheet and to them, cash flow meant simply the description of what happened on a daily basis – that is to say much money flowed in and little flowed out. In my memory flashes a melange of images from those years. They were particularly astonishing to me, as I had managed to go through the Beatles years with almost no exposure to popular music or rock and roll, but with a decent introduction to classical music.

Almost on my first day at Polydor, I was asked to attend a negotiation with the manager of that great rock and roll band The Who, the charming but tragic figure of Kit Lambert. Son of the English composer, Constant Lambert, charismatic and with a great 'ear', he battled with drug addiction and died young in 1981.

I knocked on the Managing Director's door of their office in Stratford Place in the West End of London and all I could hear was a large amount of crashing and tinkling. On opening the door, I found the Managing

Director, a Dutchman called Freddie Haayen, and Kit Lambert wrestling each other on the floor. After a few minutes they got up, said 'hello' and we got down to business. I never knew then nor do I now, what was going on in that office and, in a similarly ignorant fashion, I drafted many record contracts without any clear idea of the commercial realities of the record business. But at least I could write and in the executive ranks of the record business in those days that was a considerable achievement and gave one 'guru' status.

In those early days, with such chaos everywhere, it was easy for someone with a legal background and a reasonable talent for getting on with people to make good progress up the legal ladder. I found out how to deal with one of the most notorious managers, Don Arden, who was well known for threatening violence if not worse to executives. I treated him as a gentleman, which he found so surprising that he always treated me as one. I learned how to deal with Stevo, one of the legendary managers of the punk scene. When he threatened during our contract negotiation to go out on the window ledge above Bond Street and not come in until I agreed the point, I closed the window and locked it. He lasted about 5 minutes, before he begged to come in and we came to an amicable agreement. I slowly brought a certain discipline and intellectual rigour to the legal and business affairs department and built it up into a respectable division within the group, while also beginning to serve on various industry committees.

In due course I was promoted to Senior Legal Adviser of the UK company and eventually General Counsel of PolyGram. In this capacity, there was a lot of fun to be had doing very interesting acquisitions. The Decca Record Company was bought in 1979 for a ludicrously paltry amount which paid back within two or three years. Its artists included Joan Sutherland, Pavarotti, George Solti and their back catalogues. It had been built up from bankruptcy by the legendary Sir Edward Lewis (reputedly one of the first leading businessmen in Britain to have an official wife and an official mistress). The defence electronics and other businesses were bought by Ernest Harrison of Racal. It employed sound engineers who created some of the greatest classical recordings of all time and without whom no leading classical artist would have ever recorded anything.

John Heyman acting for Chris Blackwell, sold us Island Records. John miraculously recovered from an almost fatal car accident and was pinned together with all kinds of metal. He is also particularly deaf. His patience for negotiation is therefore somewhat limited. 'Do you want to buy this company for US$300 million?'. After a lot of humming and hawing and iffings and buttings the answer was 'yes'. 'Right I would like to draft the contract right now'. 'You must be joking'. 'No. Right now' and he would not be dissuaded.

I pointed out that I hadn't drafted this kind of agreement for 10 years and I doubted whether he had ever drafted such an agreement. Nevertheless, he was not to be put off. We sat down at seven in the evening. I asked him who the selling entity was 'Pardon?', he asked. After repeating this five times we got to clause 1. 'Clause 1,' I said. 'Pardon?', he said and so it went on for five hours. At the end we did sign an agreement on the understanding that if there were any mistakes in it, we could each put it right the next day. Although the agreement had been checked innumerable times by both myself and my colleagues on the Board of PolyGram, it was found the next day that a bit of the formula had been omitted in the final draft and, as a result, we had agreed to pay £30 million more than we wanted. I rang John immediately. He was already laughing and let us off the hook. The 80s boom had arrived with a vengeance.

In Los Angeles we stayed at the rock and roll fraternity's favourite hotel – The Sunset Marquis Hotel and Villas in West Hollywood. We shuttled to and fro with the lawyers acting for Jerry Moss and Herb Alpert who sold us A&M records for US$500 million in 1989. In the course of these negotiations I met Jerrold (Jerry) Perenchio who was performing the John Heyman role for Jerry Moss and Herb Alpert. Starting as an agent at MCA, Perenchio had very successfully bought and sold Embassy Pictures and Television, promoted Mohammed Ali fights and subsequently went on to build up the biggest and most successful Spanish language television company in the United States – Univision. He is one of the great unsung movers and shakers of the entertainment world and will feature later in the story.

All these acquisitions, apart from being a lot of fun and building up the assets of PolyGram on a world-wide basis, taught me the lesson that in most cases, when you acquire entertainment assets, they seem expensive at the time and such acquisitions are subject to much criticism, but in retrospect usually turn out to be extremely good deals. However, the fun of legal and business affairs is a limited attraction. Anyone with any sinews wants to try their hand at doing the stuff themselves, at being a businessman, at being stretched in new ways.

David Hockman joined PolyGram the same year as I did – 1975. He was a barrister by training, tall, portly, laughing, smart, friendly and loveable. He has been and remains a great friend. He had come from Dick James' music publishing company to join PolyGram in the legal department. He lasted less than a year as a lawyer and then went to join PolyGram's publishing arm, Chappel & Co. Ltd.

In the great tidy up years of the early 1980s, when a new management of PolyGram had to clear up the mess left by PolyGram Pictures and the heady years of the 1970s, David was asked by the then Managing Director of PolyGram's UK operations, David Fine, to put into some kind of shape PolyGram's UK film, television and other similar activities as well as setting up a home video company. One thing was very clear to Hockman – he was not going to get any films for a video operation from PolyGram Pictures and would have to find other sources of material.

About that time, as we were seeing a lot of each other socially, we began to talk about what could be done to plug this hole in the video plan. Slowly I began to work with David and we figured out some temporary and some longer term fixes. One of the temporary fixes was to go to the film markets that take place three times a year – at the Cannes Film Festival, Milan and Los Angeles – to acquire some feature films for the UK home video market. Secondly, we could create some content ourselves using our music company resources – that is to say, some in-concert films or long form music videos of some kind, yet to be determined. In the long term, we thought we might be able to convince our management, provided the video operation was successful, to ease PolyGram back into feature films (but David and I kept that very secret between ourselves).

And so we began to work together.

Buying movies for home video release in those days was not a very sophisticated process. You would catch the sales agent on their way to Cannes in London. Generally they would have a portfolio of films in the form of 'one sheets' in a book.

'What's this?' we'd ask.

'A cowboy type movie'.

'How much?'.

'£10,000'.

'Too much'.

'What's the next one?'.

'Oh, it's a sort of horror film'.

'How much?'.

'£10,000'.

'Who's in it?'.

'No one you've ever heard of'.

'Okay I'll take a cowboy film and the horror film for £15,000'.

'Deal,'

and so on.

Having got the plan approved to go and buy rights for the UK, I accompanied David on our first foray to the Cannes Film Festival. We had never been to Cannes and didn't know the MO. We rented a Fiat 500 at Nice Airport and drove towards Cannes in the pouring rain. Neither of us could navigate and we ended up at La Napoule. Finding Cannes, we dripped our way round town for 10 days with £1 million burning a hole in our pocket. Eventually we found that the biggest game in town was run by two Israelis. It was called Cannon. They were called Menachem

Golan and Yoram Globus. With some trepidation we went to see them in their corner suite at the Carlton Hotel, where there were many busty blondes and a sumptuous buffet. We said we were there to buy their entire slate for the UK for home video. Little did we know that the day before Golan and Globus had sold all their product to someone else for £8 million. However Menachem let us get our speech out and eventually asked how much we were willing to pay. 'Listen to this...,' we confidently said, 'We are willing to pay, not a quarter of a million, not a half, but a whole million pounds for your slate'. After laughing uproariously, they patted us on the knee and said, 'Boys, if you want groceries there's a shop on the corner!'.

Another experience comes to mind. After we'd made a number of long form videos – bands in concert for home video use – we went to try and sell the rights in Cannes. After a tremendous amount of fruitless effort we were thrilled, eventually, to sell the rights to Japan for what seemed to us a large sum of money. A very nice Japanese executive who bought it from us was called Noboyuki Idei. He currently runs Sony world-wide.

In due course, David and I convinced David Fine to allow us to set up a proper production company in the UK to make long form music videos. It was terribly exciting. We called it PolyGram Music Video or PMV. We filmed any band that could move, shake their bums or play any kind of instrument. What we were really looking for was some kind of music-led visual entertainment that was more than just an in-concert. To that end we made a couple of long form music videos. One was featuring the then hot band ABC and entitled *Man Trap* directed by Julien Temple and the other was one entitled *Now Voyager* starring Barry Gibb.

Neither of these set the world alight commercially or creatively and that was the end for us and for the world of the long form music video.

Our next major venture was to participate in the beginning of sell-through video. In the early days video feature films were sold to rental shops for a relatively large amount of money and the rental shop would then rent them out and make their profit that way. However, in the early 1980s, Paul Levinson in the United Kingdom pioneered the concept of selling videos direct to the public at retail. This took off in a big way and is the bedrock on which the sell-through video business in its current form of DVD is set.

David Hockman and I formed a joint venture with UK property developer Gerald Ronson's company, Heron, which had diversified from property into feature films without much success. They owned some feature films, we owned some other programming and a UK distribution organisation which we put together in a joint venture called Channel 5 Video. This was very successful, as was PolyGram Video, and both ventures gave David Hockman and myself some credibility as managers as well as lawyers and deal makers.

And so it was that in our 1985 budget for PolyGram Music Video, which I have before me as I write, I find that in addition to planning to do 14 in-concert films and four 'visualised records', there was also provision to do two 'high budget music-based films' at £1.5 million each.

The moment this budget was approved. The die was cast. Here began the story of PolyGram Filmed Entertainment.

Private Investigations

Heavily disguised as a long form music video 'with words', albeit with a high budget, we decided to enter the feature film business. We wanted no downside risk at all. We therefore decided to tailor this movie to be attractive to the video market. I spoke to the only person I knew in the film business – Nigel Dick. Nigel had been a commissioner of pop promotional videos at PolyGram in the UK before starting to direct promotional videos himself and in 1985 had moved back to Los Angeles. I rang Nigel and said I wanted a movie with a chase, an explosion, a shock and a girl in it. He said 'No problem,' and gave me a pitch called *Private Investigations* which covered most of this ground. I asked him if he knew any writers. He said he knew John Dahl (who subsequently went on to direct *Red Rock West* (1992) and *The Last Seduction* (1994)) and his writing partner David Warfield (who later married Callie Khourie who wrote *Thelma and Louise*). Did he know any producers? He said he was working for a man called Steve Golin and his partner Joni Sighvatsson. David Hockman and I headed to Los Angeles to meet Nigel, Steve and Joni in the least expensive room we could get at the Beverly Hills Hotel and four months later *Private Investigations* went into production starring Ray Sharkey and Martin Balsam.

I have had frightening moments as a baby producer – when, for instance, I made *Pavarotti in Concert at the Albert Hall*. This was a joint venture with the BBC and the total budget was about £50,000. Five minutes before the concert was supposed to go out live, I was called backstage because Pavarotti wouldn't go on. The problem was solved by the more experienced orchestra manager, but I still remember the trembling, sinking feeling at the time. As *Private Investigations* went into production with the enormous budget of around $800,000, I was beside myself with fear and anxiety. Every night at midnight London time, I would confer with Steve Golin on the 'phone. In the first week he admitted there was a slight problem. The slight problem turned out to be that Ray Sharkey had been arrested. Could we get him out of jail? 'Normally,' said Steve, 'we could,' but there was another slight problem. 'What was that?' I asked. Sharkey had jumped bail before on a similar drugs charge. My Pavarotti experience came into its own. I shouted and railed at Steve but underneath I did not panic and indeed, someway or another, the film came together and according to its lights was fine. Samuel Goldwyn Jnr, through his company the Samuel Goldwyn Company, bought the international rights for about $1 million and David and I set off to Los Angeles to sell the United States rights.

Fate led us up the steps of the glorious Thalberg Building on what was then the MGM lot, but now belongs to Sony. We were ushered into a screening room, having delivered the rushes of *Private Investigations* to the projectionist. In the room, amongst others, was Alan Ladd Jnr who at that time was running the studio. Neither of us knew that he was famous for not saying a word, whether through shyness or otherwise. He sat through what we had to show him and left the room without a hello or a goodbye. We collected our films from the projectionist and as we took the little handcart down the steps of the Thalberg Building, the cans fell off all over the place and rolled to the bottom of the steps where there was an MGM commissionaire. He laughed himself stupid at these two Englishmen chasing their cans of film all over the Thalberg lot and said that he'd heard of producers 'schlepping' their movies from one studio to another, but he had never seen it before.

A very depressed Kuhn and Hockman left the lot, film in hand. About an hour later, we had a phone call saying that MGM would buy the North American rights for $1 million. We were ecstatic. Here we were: proper film producers who had made nearly $1 million profit on their first film which obviously must have been brilliant for it to be bought up so quickly by Sam Goldwyn and MGM. Little did we know that MGM had some troublesome video deal, where they needed to push rubbish movies in order to prevent their co-venturer getting their hands on MGM's good movies and that was the reason for them buying our films. Sometimes the naive view of life is the best, but needless to say, for all its faults, *Private Investigations* retains a special place in my heart and marks a turning point in my life, as there was no doubt now what my ambition was – to build from such small beginnings, a world-wide film studio based out of London.

3
Commitment and relationships

In the early 1980s, PolyGram went through a baptism of fire. As mentioned earlier, Philips brought in one of their own, a bulky bald Dutchman called Jan Timmer who had been running their South African operation. He knew nothing about the music business but came to form a close business partnership with someone who had been a star manager of the music business in that country, David Fine. David had run Gallo, one of South Africa's foremost record businesses, and was now running PolyGram UK.

Initially, Fine came over to sort out the disastrous UK operations of PolyGram and subsequently rose to run world-wide operations under Timmer, eventually succeeding him. On meeting Timmer, one could easily underestimate him. He looked like everyone's idea of a Dutch burgher, with his enormous frame, significant weight problem, unfashionable dress style and a jaw that put Mussolini's in the shade. After a very unpromising start, he turned out to be a legendary leader and, indeed, the saviour of the music industry. As a manager, his forte was the big strategic plan and he had no time for the details of running a business. He left that to David Fine.

Jan Timmer was thrust into the driving seat of a large world-wide organisation requiring strategic partnerships, but had no experience of large organisations and little sensible advice on acquiring such partners. Until David Fine came along, there was no one to do the nuts and bolts running of the business and his strategic decision making rested more on impulse and feeling than on mature consideration and quiet thought.

An early, but stunning example of his lack of experience came when a proposed merger with Warner Brothers' Music Operations seemed likely.

The charismatic head of Warner Communications, Steve Ross, had captivated and charmed Timmer. As a result of this, a plan was hatched to merge the operations of PolyGram and Warner. The first the employees knew of this was when key management of both companies were flown to an anonymous hotel outside Heathrow Airport, where beaming and self-congratulatory management from both companies announced the merger of these hitherto arch-enemies in the music business. PolyGram employees sat on one side of the room and Warner employees sat on the other, ignoring each other. Warners had much the better part of the deal and the PolyGram employees were left feeling badly treated and uninformed. As it happened, despite the assurances that Warners could see the proposed joint venture through the relevant American anti-trust authorities, this did not happen and the deal fell apart.

Those early years saw a transformation in the stature of Jan Timmer. He became the main proponent of the introduction of the audio compact disc as the saviour of the record industry in general and PolyGram in particular. Without his dogged determination and immovability of purpose, it is doubtful whether PolyGram would have survived and the record business would have kissed the prospect of annihilation.

Jan travelled the globe to make sure that CD was established as a world standard and that record companies came on board to support the new carrier with content. As early as 1983, it was clear to PolyGram, which owned the first CD pressing plant, that the new carrier was taking off. Projections for number of units sold per player were overtaken by the reality. However, it was hard to convince outsiders that a revolution was beginning that would transform the fortunes of the record industry and PolyGram.

Timmer had to find a partner for Philips in PolyGram and I accompanied him on several of his trips – and what trips they were!

At the time, the giant of the entertainment business, particularly in Los Angeles, was considered to be MCA. The boss of MCA was the legendary Lew Wasserman and his henchman, the acerbic Sid Sheinberg. The PolyGram team arrived in LA the day before a meeting had been arranged with Lew and Sid to discuss the potential acquisition of a 50 per cent ownership interest in PolyGram by MCA. The evening we arrived, we checked into a small unobtrusive hotel in West Hollywood. A message was waiting for Timmer. Lew Wasserman had invited him to his home for dinner. We begged Jan not to go, as we suspected a softening up effort. Jan was entirely dismissive of our suspicions and set off. Next morning at breakfast he expounded at length at what a charming man Lew Wasserman was, what a charming wife he had, what a wonderful house with wonderful art. We felt very nervous. A fleet of black limos arrived to take us to the headquarters of MCA in the valley. The black limos reminded me of nothing so much as the Zyl limousine that would collect heads of state from Eastern European countries and take them from Moscow airport to the Kremlin to hear their fate. MCA's headquarters were in a large black tower block known unsurprisingly as 'The Black Tower' on the Universal Lot in Burbank.

We were ushered into a meeting room on the top floor where there were dozens of MCA executives together with the obligatory coffee, croissants, cookies and other breakfast foods beloved of Hollywood entertainment companies. After a little milling around, Wasserman and Sheinberg grabbed Timmer and indicated that he should join them in a very small side conference room. Timmer hauled me along and the four of us ended up in this little room away from the mob.

While Lew Wasserman examined his nails carefully, Sid Sheinberg came to the point at once. Effectively, he intimated that they had looked over the PolyGram books, thought it was a shit company with no prospects, but would, however, be interested in buying a half interest for a low figure, but of course the management (i.e Timmer) would have to go.

This was not a method of operation familiar to European management and I had some difficulty keeping my jaw from dropping to the floor. Timmer very calmly rose, thanked them for their time and we left.

Michael Eisner at Disney 'passed' on buying into PolyGram. Martin Davis at Paramount/Gulf and Western politely refused to buy and eventually we were left with groupings backed by venture capital funds. At this time of general depression, Wolfgang Hix, (then General Counsel of PolyGram) came into his own. While appearing to agree with everything Jan Timmer said and every deal he proposed doing, (among others there was a long discussion with a group led by Alan Hirshfield, former boss of Columbia Pictures and thereafter an investment banker, and including, surprisingly Trevor Chinn of the Lex Group in the UK), Hix would find reasons why it was not possible to agree to certain terms proposed by the other side. As a result, every avenue seemed closed off and eventually Timmer got fed up and convinced the Philips Board that they were an old and proud company and should not have to accept completely ridiculous terms to get a partner in PolyGram, let alone have partners which were not their equals. The result was that Philips bit the bullet, did not sell an interest in PolyGram and allowed Timmer to find a way out of the mess.

In due course, David Fine's magnificent re-engineering of the group brought PolyGram from the ranks of the worst-managed companies to that of the best-managed companies in the music business; Timmer's visionary leadership in the introduction of the compact disc brought untold riches to the record industry and to PolyGram and eventually, PolyGram's balance sheet propped up Philips as the parent company went through hard times in the 1980s and early 1990s.

As well as giving me a wonderful experience in high-up corporate management, it introduced me to key players in the film business in Hollywood.

The new spirit of optimism that Timmer and Fine engendered in PolyGram set the scene for PolyGram to be willing to take on my plan to enter the movie business – but not without a major scare.

Having established my power base in PolyGram through my relationship with David Fine and Jan Timmer, it soon became clear that tensions existed between the two men even as the prosperity of PolyGram grew. David Fine felt that much of the turnaround should be credited to him as the day-to-day nuts-and-bolts manager of a very complex worldwide organisation. Jan Timmer (although he would never express such a sentiment in public or in private) felt that nuts-and-bolts managers could be found relatively easily and deserved little special credit.

Determination and vision were required. So even though, when Timmer left to rejoin Philips, of which he eventually became Chief Executive, and gave David Fine the job of President of PolyGram, he began looking round for a visionary leader to succeed Fine and found one at CBS Records in France – a French-born, American-educated executive called Alain Lévy.

DAVID FINE

I believe this tension between Timmer and Fine led to a kind of taking sides where one was either a 'Fine man' or a 'Timmer man'. Rightly or wrongly (and again this was never expressed openly) I felt that David Fine, whom hitherto I had believed to be a very close friend, thought I was in the Timmer camp and ceased to be a close ally. It was thus in 1987 that I was made President of the vaguely named 'New Business Division'. Its remit was to look after stuff that no one else was interested in. Jan Timmer's new obsession (after CD Audio) was CD-Interactive and CD-Video. Both of these seemed to most people at PolyGram and Philips to be mad ventures into untried technology. However, no-one could gainsay the miracle worker Jan Timmer and I was given responsibility for overseeing PolyGram's involvement with these activities, together with various other unimportant and tedious PolyGram operations. I spent a useless 12 months in Los Angeles bored out of my mind, ostensibly looking after the CD Interactive operation called American Interactive Media and trying to build on the financial success of *Private Investigations* and get a film company going. I decided to cut my losses and come back to the UK.

I saw David Fine and said I was unhappy and unless we could find something for me to do I would leave. I fully expected David to say, 'Don't leave', but he just kept quiet. I went home to think about handing in my notice, but the more I thought about it, the more I felt I had not spent all this time at PolyGram to give up now on the vision of building a film studio, and came back to work in my ill-defined role, carefully avoiding any conflict with David Fine or the subject of my future.

This patience on my part turned out to be the right course of action. In 1989 Alain Lévy who had by now turned PolyGram's French operation from terrible losses to a company which had a French market share in excess of 30 per cent, as expected was brought onto the board of PolyGram as the clearly designated heir of Jan Timmer and successor to David Fine.

The first time I had met Alain Lévy had been in his office at PolyGram France. Whatever the meeting was about, the only thing I remember clearly is that throughout, he sat shoeless on the floor, scratching his long curly hair and glancing around the room through fingerprint smeared glasses, smoking prodigiously. We laughed a lot and he was very smart. In the strange way that sometimes happens, a relationship began between us that was close and which lasts to this day. Whatever faults he had, his most important attributes were a first class brain, a complete commitment to truth in all things and a loyalty to friends which is rare in our business.

But the end of the 1980s saw a strange tension in my life. On the one hand I had a really boring unappreciated job at PolyGram with a plan to build a film division, but on the face of it, no hope of doing so under David Fine. On the other hand, I had the prospect of a new visionary coming in to PolyGram to take over where Timmer had left off, someone who I felt intuitively would understand and support me in the task ahead.

And so the 1980s came to a close on a bitter-sweet note.

ALAIN LÉVY

4
The strategy unfolds

Control vs creativity

The more I thought about the problems of setting up and running a successful entertainment company, the more it seemed to me that the key issues were firstly, how to control a creative company, imposing financial disciplines but not stifling creativity; and secondly, how to squeeze every penny of value out of the product produced, in order to make the numbers work. On both counts, I felt that the system pioneered by Steve Ross at Warner Communications and copied by PolyGram in the 1980s was a very good solution. In short it was as follows:

On the creative side, it was not part of central management's role to produce content. It should back good, creative people and give them a good deal of autonomy, provided they stick to financial disciplines. In the music business, this became known as the label system. For example, in the classical division there were three creative units: Deutsche Grammophon, Philips and Decca. All these had strong management with different tastes. They were given a budget and they got on with producing good classical records. On the pop side we had, among others, Polydor Records, A&M, Island, Mercury and several other labels. Again, they usually had a strong creative management, who were left to get on with the business of attracting talent and making successful records. In return for this autonomy, they had to observe strict financial disciplines.

In order to maximise profitability, it was essential to be in control of your own marketing and world-wide distribution. It was clear to me that if you sold off rights for most of the world, you would benefit by having the income at once guaranteed and up front, but at the end of the day, you would lose out because you were not in control of your own marketing and you could never maximise profitability.

I thought it was possible to apply these principles to the movie business. On the face of it this was a big challenge. Of all industries, Hollywood is perhaps the most centralised. The power to 'green light' movies is the most jealously guarded right and is usually vested in Hollywood. The world-wide distribution of movies is guided from Hollywood. The focus of Hollywood studios is very much North America and, whatever they say even to this day, the international exploitation of movies is not the prime focus of those studios. I felt we could do better and so it was that even as early as 1988, long before my film plan was approved, I started sewing the seeds of this plan and testing elements of this theory. I looked around for producers or 'labels' I had confidence in and I began to explore taking on more of the distribution risks and rewards. The first two labels I took an interest in, were Propaganda Films in Los Angeles and Working Title Films in London and the first tentative steps into taking more risk and reward in the international distribution side, was the establishment in 1989 of Manifesto Film Sales – PolyGram's foreign sales company charged with selling movies in territories outside North America.

Propaganda Films

The first producers I met in Los Angeles were Sigurjon 'Joni' Sighvatsson and Steve Golin, founders of Propaganda Films who produced *Private Investigations* – my first film.

JONI SIGHVATSSON

Joni was Icelandic. Tall, skinny, neurotic and always looking 15 years younger than his age, he left Iceland in 1978 to study at the graduate film studies programme at the University of Southern California on a Fullbright Scholarship. It was at the American Film Institute, which he went on to after USC Film School, that he met Steve Golin. Steve was a New Yorker, short, Jewish, equable. After attending film school at NYU, he worked as an assistant photographer, before joining the AFI.

STEVE GOLIN

The two of them started to produce low budget movies, the first of which *Hard Rock Zombies* (1984) was made for US$300,000 and the second *American Drive-In* (1985) for US$400,000.

To pay the bills, they started producing music videos directed by friends of theirs, such as John Dahl (subsequently a director of note) and David Warfield.

Immediately after producing *Private Investigations,* the two of them formed Propaganda Films. Among their early partner/directors were David Fincher (later to direct *Alien 3, Seven, The Game* and *Fight Club*), Dominic Sena (*Kalifornia, Gone in 60 Seconds* and *Swordfish*), Michael Bay (*Bad Boys, The Rock, Armageddon* and *Pearl Harbour*) and a little later on, Spike Jonze (*Being John Malkovich*).

I was attracted to Steve and Joni's energy and hipness, together with the great creative people with whom they were associated.

We soon agreed to a partnership and I got permission to test the water in the relationship with them, by buying 49 per cent of their company in January 1988, for a total cost of $3.25 million.

Using the money injected by PolyGram into their company, they were soon established in Frank Israel-designed offices in West Hollywood and producing the first of several low budget, low risk (and, as it turned out, low interest) movies, including the *Blue Iguana* with Dylan McDermott and Jessica Harper, directed by John Lafia, *Fear, Anxiety and Depression* directed by Todd Solondz (later to direct *Welcome to the Doll House* and *Happiness*) and *Kill Me Again* with Val Kilmer and Joanne Whalley, directed by John Dahl.

It turned out to be a good way to get one's eye in on the film-making business and the difficulty of turning good ideas into good films – but at acceptable risk.

Working Title Films

Another cornerstone company was Working Title Films. Tim Bevan was tall with a diffident, shy character which belied his open features. At first he often came across as arrogant, but in truth, like Steve Golin, was down to earth, loyal, hardworking and totally reliable. He had partnered in the early 1980s with Sarah Radclyffe.

Apart from producing music videos to earn a crust, Tim had made *My Beautiful Launderette* in 1985, which had been a great critical success. Tim had met Steve and Joni and they in turn mentioned that Tim might be interested in getting together with me at PolyGram. After some discussion, we came to the conclusion that the best way to test out a relationship (given that there was no music video production unit similar to Propaganda, at Working Title) was to do a joint venture in television. In July 1988, we took a 49 per cent interest in Working Title Television, which neither Tim nor I were really interested in except as the beginning of a relationship. The first project was a co-production with Channel 4 called *Smack and Thistle*.

Tim and I both agreed that, until UK producers could spend more time on making a script and a movie work, than they did on trying to get a movie made, there was little hope of moving forward. It took some time for him to get the development slate at Working Title back on track and, in the interim, the result was a slew of bad and unsuccessful movies, such as *For Queen and Country, Diamond Skulls, Fools of Fortune, London Kills Me* and *Map of the Human Heart*.

In the case of both Propaganda Films and Working Title Films, I had anticipated a significant wind-up period and felt that it was my responsibility to ensure that, in the event of a period of extended failure, we would survive. This involved combining significant international pre-sales and tax structures that would alleviate the inevitable losses and make them sustainable. At the time we bought into Working Title, Tim Bevan had a third partner, Graham Bradstreet, a clever but totally chaotic (in the managerial sense) New Zealander with an accountancy background. Together with my Chief Financial Officer, Malcolm Ritchie, they set about financing our movies through a German film fund, which meant that 10 per cent of the budget of movies was covered before we began – that was the good news. The bad news was that Tim and Sarah had relied on Graham to look after all the administrative, tax and other affairs of Working Title prior to us getting involved and, let us say, his interests lay elsewhere. The result was that, while I had anticipated that any independent production company would have its affairs in a certain amount of disorder, nothing prepared either Malcolm or myself for the total chaos within Working Title which took several years to sort out.

TIM BEVAN (SEATED) AND ERIC FELLNER

Manifesto Film Sales

Having found my first two production labels, I now began thinking about the international sales business.

From the earliest days, I had seen how small independent sales agents who sold English language movies in the international non-USA markets, could often make an attractive margin with little risk. In addition, their general knowledge of the international market place and the value of films to the distributors to whom they were selling, was a valuable source of intelligence for any producer. I soon felt that, if we were to take on any additional risk in film-making, the best arena in which to take on such risk was the international sales business.

It was obviously very important to find the right person to lead such an operation. Tim Bevan suggested the name of Wendy Palmer. Wendy came from New Zealand and had managed foreign sales at George Harrison's company, Handmade Films, for a number of years, until she was made redundant. She had then taken the idea of setting up an independent sales company to Tim Bevan who liked it, but was unable to back it at the time. Eventually she took a job working for Stewart Till at Sky Broadcasting. Wendy is one of those people who never feels very happy in a large organisation, so when I approached her in early 1989, she had already decided to leave Sky and did not need much persuading.

Obviously she did not know what was in store by way of accommodation. Working Title found a tiny space for her in already overcrowded offices in Livonia Street, Soho. This became so chaotic, noisy, argumentative and inefficient, that eventually, I had to agree to them moving to a two room office in Wardour Street. Wendy operated with her assistant, Caroline Burton, and the marketing director, John Dury, in premises where, in order to have a meeting in the bigger office, chairs had to be taken out and a cupboard shifted. However, the small team could see everybody coming in and out of Soho through their window as well as keep an eye on Working Title. They left for their first film market in Milan at the end of 1989 with two Working Title films (*Chicago Joe and the Showgirl* and *Fools of Fortune*) and two Propaganda films (*Wild at Heart* and *Daddy's Dyin'... Whose got the Will?*) in their pre-sales bag.

This little team not only proved the wisdom of getting into the foreign sales business, by greatly exceeding the best sales estimates at their first market, but also by giving us all a presence in the international market – a presence which was a nice mixture of promising movies, lots of booze and an atmosphere of fun and optimism. Manifesto's first major success came when *Wild at Heart* won the Palm d'Or at their first Cannes Film Festival in 1990.

Wild at Heart

David Lynch is generally thought of as being at the weird end of American directors. I myself went to see *Blue Velvet* with a group of friends without really concentrating on which film we were about to watch. I vaguely thought that it was something to do with horses and Elizabeth Taylor and so was somewhat surprised. His TV series *Twin Peaks* must have been one of the most outré TV series ever to appear on American network television, while *Eraser Head* (despite what the critics say) is so out there as to be almost unwatchable.

In person, he always reminded me most of Stan Laurel, both physically and in his mannerisms, such as scratching his head in a Laurelesque way. Steve Golin and his friend, Monty Montgomery, got to know David Lynch in the late 1980s and we all became infatuated with the script for *Wild at Heart*, based on a novel by Barry Gifford. Despite the critical success of *Blue Velvet*, it took some time to set up the production, as it was not exactly a mainstream movie. In the end, a first rate cast was assembled, including Nicolas Cage (before he was Nicolas Cage), Laura Dern, Willem Dafoe, Crispin Glover, Isabella Rossellini and Harry Dean Stanton, among others. The final movie was pretty violent, but more extreme footage was left on the cutting room floor of Lucas Ranch in Northern California, where the film was edited.

Courtesy Propaganda Films

DAVID LYNCH

It was in a state of some excitement, that we learned that the film was invited to premier at the Cannes Film Festival in May 1990. Apart from David Lynch and Isabella Rossellini, Nick Cage and Laura Dern came to Cannes to promote the film. Our little foreign sales company, Manifesto, were beside themselves with excitement at being put in the limelight and did a most marvellous marketing and promotional job. Somewhat unusually, for whatever reason, the cast, as well as ourselves, were at the Palais de Festival in Cannes for the last night when the winner of the Palme d'Or was to be announced.

However, no one had told us that as the phrase *Wild at Heart* was impossible to translate into French, an alternative title, *Sailor et Lula*, had been given to the French version. When it was announced that the winner was *Sailor et Lula*, we all looked at each other and wondered which film this was. Once the Director General of the Festival, the autocratic Gilles Jacob, had made it clear that that meant us, a most wonderful melee developed to get onto the stage to accept the prize. After the prize-giving ceremony the Festival authorities informed us that there would be an *homage* to a famous director and we were to come back after that for the official dinner in the Palais. They would send cars to pick us up. I despatched a minion to organise an impromptu dinner at the Carlton Hotel on the Croisette and after press interviews and such, we made our way there. Sitting tucking into our hastily arranged dinner was Harvey Weinstein, the famous founder of Miramax films. How he had found out about the dinner and why he was there, history has yet to reveal. The minion had also found an accordionist on the Croisette and hired him to come play to the troops. Unfortunately, he could only play *Happy Birthday to You* and proceeded to do so for the next two hours.

Eventually a fleet of Citroens flying the flag of the Festival arrived to take us to the Palais, where there were thousands of people gathered around the famous red-carpeted steps. We walked up, bowing left and right, as movie royalty should, but once inside the doors, French bureaucracy took over. A gendarme informed us that we were not on the list and couldn't come in. The more we insisted that we had won the Palme d'Or and demanded to come in, the more steadfast became his refusal. I, for one, had decided I would stay until morning as there was no way I was going to walk sheepishly back down those triumphant steps looking desolate and pathetic.

The situation was saved by Isabella Rossellini, who knew the Cannes system inside out from the many visits she had paid there with her famous director father. Moreover, she spoke excellent French, that ultimate Cannes passport, and so within a short period of time, we were led up the stairs to a vast dining hall where at least a thousand (or so it seemed to us) burghers of Cannes were tucking into a fine dinner. The good news was that a table was waiting for us but there were only four places laid. Admitting defeat, we left the cast to get on with it and headed off to the terrace of the Majestic Hotel to have a drink.

After a short while, the terrace filled up with more and more friends and I had foolishly given in my credit card. By the time I recovered it at 4.00am, we had probably been joined by some thousand people and had drunk several crates of Dom Perignon. For several months later I dreaded the credit card account and the inevitable shame-faced explanations to my superiors. When it did come the gods had smiled on me. The account showed I owed only $200, which would probably have paid for one bottle. For a very short period of time I wondered whether I should own up and admit that the bill must have been much higher than this. I thought of all the years that I and others had been ripped off appallingly by every hotel on the Croisette and I did not to do the honourable thing. I can't say I have had any pangs of conscience since then.

Wild at Heart marked an important moment in the development of PolyGram Films. It showed that we could compete with the best at festivals, that we could work with great film-makers and talent and that we could win prizes.

However, I learned that all this does not translate into box office success. The movie, despite being extremely well received critically, did very little business at the box office.

5
Building a studio

PolyGram's advantages

By mid 1991, the development phase had come to a conclusion. The result of having made eight pictures in the period 1989 to mid-1991 was pretty much a break-even, financially. The individual profit and loss accounts varied significantly, as did the budgets. The lowest budget movie was the Working Title film *London Kills Me* and the largest was $16 million for Vincent Ward's *Map of the Human Heart*. There were some profitable movies such as Working Title's *Drop Dead Fred,* which had a US box office of $15 million and a negative cost of $6.4 million, as well as some awful duds. *Ruby* directed by John McKenzie cost $9.1 million and only grossed $1 million at the US box office.

In 1991 itself, we began production on Sidney Lumet's *Close to Eden* starring Melanie Griffiths, Bernard Rose's *Candyman* and John Dahl's *Red Rock West,* once again with Nicolas Cage. Of these films, *Candyman* was the most successful, taking some US$25 million at the American box office, while *Red Rock West* was both modestly profitable and a critical success.

It was in January of 1991, that Alain Lévy finally ascended to the presidency of PolyGram and my confidence grew that our plans for building a European-based studio would get the green light. Alain enunciated at the PolyGram Annual Convention in April how he viewed PolyGram's future as a European entertainment powerhouse, encompassing movies, music and television. At my suggestion, Alain had studied the disastrous history of PolyGram Pictures and had read the best book on how building a studio from scratch can go wrong (*My Indecision is Final* by Jake Eberts and Terry Illott).

I always thought that if we had a half decent plan, we had a few built-in advantages that would give us a reasonable shot at being successful.

A third or more of all revenues from movies came from home video. Home video involved the shipping of bits of plastic to the public through a sophisticated distribution system on a world-wide basis. Unlike most film studios at the time, we had a world-wide distribution system capable of distributing bits of plastic to the public, but we were only using it for one bit of plastic – the music carrier.

Secondly, the movie business required a significant amount of capital, but PolyGram's cash flow ran into hundreds of millions of dollars a year and significantly exceeded any possible requirement of its core music business.

Thirdly, through our music business, we had developed the label system, which combines creative autonomy with financial discipline – a management technique that I thought could be well adapted to the film business.

Fourthly, we had by this time developed a very strong world-wide management team. At its core, we had the best bean counter in the music business, a Dutchman called Jan Cook. On the music side, the team included such people as Roger Ames (currently Head of Warner Music), Norman Cheng, the best manager in the Far East and responsible for all PolyGram's Far East operations based in Hong Kong, my friend David Hockman, who by now ran our music publishing operations and Richard Constant, one of the best General Counsel in any entertainment company.

Alain felt that we would develop even better management giving them the opportunity to be both music and film managers and this certainly proved true. Both he and I felt certain that when the compact disc reached maturity (in the late 1990's) the music business would have significant growth problems and we would need an add-on business. Lastly, we knew that in the entertainment business, mixing international content and national local content led to the strongest market position and we felt we could do in film what we had done in music, which was to successfully blend the two.

So, together with the help of Malcolm Ritchie on the figures and Jill Tandy on the legal side, I started to prepare a 10 year plan to present to the board of PolyGram and the board of Philips. In the course of preparing the plan, I also had to anticipate being up to speed, when and if the plan was accepted. And so it was we looked at buying Nik Powell's Palace Pictures. The company was on the verge of bankruptcy. Nik needed help. It could have been an interesting art label addition to our group and had a nice little catalogue of UK rights to international films. However, despite making a loan to the company secured on its assets, we couldn't prevent it going into liquidation. We also had some fun putting together a bid for one of the London TV franchises. We managed to drive up the price and although the franchise changed hands, we were not the successful bidder, despite probably having bid the highest amount. It takes years to get into the broadcasting establishment in England! Our acquisition of the Coen brothers' film *Barton Fink* gave us the beginnings of a long term relationship with the Coens and the Palme d'Or at the Cannes Film Festival for the second year in a row.

On the 14th August Malcolm Ritchie, Jan Cook, Alain Lévy and I flew to Eindhoven in the Netherlands to present the PolyGram film plan to Jan Timmer and the Philips Board. Eindhoven is the archetypal company town, but since those days most of Philips has decamped to Amsterdam. Then, however, the buildings were all numbered (VO1 and so on), not named. The town, although surrounded by beautiful countryside, is dismal. The Philips Headquarters building is anonymous and approached through an underground garage. An elevator takes the visitor up to the ground floor, where there is a modern sculpture sitting in a pool of what looks like blood. Escalators that work only when approached exude an air of gloom and foreboding.

The Philips Board seemed to us to be made up of octogenarian Belgian and Dutch gentlemen. The boardroom was big enough for a significant sized meeting of the United Nations and the board addressed via microphone. Had I not known that Jan Timmer was going to push the thing through, the reception for our plan would have depressed the most optimistic executive. In the end Jan Timmer prevailed, the plan was approved and we were off to the races.

The plan

So what was this plan that I presented to the Philips board? In short, it was to build, over a five year period, a studio without a 'lot'. Production would be in the hands of a number of production 'labels' between them capable of producing eight to 15 movies a year. Marketing and sales organisations would be centralised and, eventually, we would distribute our movies through augmented national PolyGram organisations, with a great degree of autonomy being given to the head of the national operations on all matters to do with distribution of our movies. In the smaller territories, we would sell films to third parties on a licence basis and we would endeavour to make some non-English language films wherever that was feasible – probably in France, Germany, Spain and Italy.

In the short term, we would hope to distribute our bigger movies through one of the existing studios in North America and our smaller movies would go through our own theatrical video and TV distribution, which we would set up immediately. In the longer term in America, we would establish our own theatrical distribution business and no longer have to depend on American studios for distribution.

In this way, we would gradually expand the number of countries where we handled our own distribution and thereby access most of the world-wide distribution margins.

Our initial plan called for a total investment cost, based on peak cash flow, of US$200 million. The plan noted that further production units and catalogues would continue to be acquired, with any specific proposals being dealt with on a case by case basis.

It was a condition of the plan being approved that I moved to Los Angeles to run things there. So I left England to set up shop in California, on the 1st January 1992.

Los Angeles

Home was a one bedroom apartment on Laurel Avenue, off Sunset Boulevard in West Hollywood. The office was a few rooms rented from our lawyers on Maple Drive in Beverly Hills.

My priorities were to ensure we had a good flow of movies, to set up our US distribution arrangements – big movies through a studio, small movies through our own distribution company, Gramercy – and slowly, step by step, to open up our own distribution countries internationally.

That meant I had to leave the international side of things in a capable pair of hands. I had been told that Stewart Till was the man. He had been working at Rupert Murdoch's Sky Television with responsibility for the acquisition of all Sky's film and entertainment products. He had started off in the advertising business, initially with Leo Burnett and thereafter, Saatchi and Saatchi. He had also spent some years with WEA Records as marketing director and with CBS Fox Video as a regional director for Northern Europe. No CV could have been more perfect for what I wanted.

From film-makers, I had heard that he read scripts immediately and gave answers promptly and had a wide ranging taste in movies from big block-busters to more art house films. After a relatively short courtship, he came in to run our international operations. Stewart himself was polit-ically adept, dapper, ambitious and sure-footed. If my instincts were right, I could concentrate on production and the US.

Jan Timmer had given me an introduction to Frank Wells, Michael Eisner's partner at Disney. It is widely thought that if Frank Wells had not died in a plane crash in 1994, Disney would be a greater company and a better place to work than it is considered today. I explained my plan to Frank Wells and almost alone among all the hot shots I met in Hollywood, he thought the idea could work and was fresh and original.

An early priority was to establish some credibility for the agencies in Los Angeles and the creative community. I went to see Jeff Berg at the ICM Agency and he suggested I meet with Jodie Foster.

Courtesy Orion

JODIE FOSTER

With some nervousness I arranged to meet Jodie for dinner at the Ivy Restaurant. When she arrived, it was hard to recognise the star of so many great movies in the slight, short, bespectacled figure. However, over dinner, it became clear that she was ambitious to produce (and not just as a vanity operation) as well as direct. We certainly hit it off enough that, within a few months, we had closed a deal with her company, Egg Pictures. We paid her overheads and gave her development money, in return for an option on all movies that she produced. Although we were to have some ups and downs over the ensuing years, she turned out to be a loyal partner and professional in every respect, never failing to attend promotional meetings with our international companies or international buyers.

I thought it best to buy out the remaining shares in Propaganda and Working Title and this was put in hand almost immediately at the beginning of 1992. I then started thinking about our bigger budget movies. We could probably get any major studio to distribute them for a fee, but that would leave an incredible risk remaining – we would have put up a large amount of money for marketing, as well as foregoing the advance we got if we sold a movie for North American. The key to getting round this problem was to get a pay TV deal – a deal with Home Box Office or Show Time, where a very large amount of money was guaranteed, provided a movie got a significant theatrical release. If one could get a pay TV deal and added on the fairly predictable video revenues, the risk in setting up a USA distribution would be much ameliorated. This was also true if we hoped to cover the downside risk of our intended smaller budget distribution company.

The problem was that, at the beginning of the 1990's, it was almost impossible to get such a pay TV deal. Fortunately our lawyer in Los Angeles, Nigel Sinclair, introduced me to Richard Northcott. Richard, a mercurial, wild and lovely man, who had made some money in the supermarket business in England, had got into very great difficulties with his US company, Nelson Entertainment, and was shutting it down and selling off its assets. One of those assets was a deal with Show Time which had several years to run, guaranteeing significant pay TV revenues for yet to be delivered movies. With the agreement of Matthew Blank at Show Time, I acquired these 'slots' and could now look to set up our own domestic distribution company.

Although I had the go-ahead to set up our own small distribution operation in North America, I was still nervous that I would not have enough movies. So I approached Tom Pollock who was then running Universal Pictures and asked him if he would be interested in joint venturing what the Americans called a 'classics' theatrical distribution operation. Tom and I had several long and informative lunches to discuss the matter. Tom had a background as one of the most powerful and respected entertainment lawyers in Los Angeles and ran Universal Studios quite successfully for a number of years, reporting to Sid Sheinberg and Lew Wasserman. The good news was that, eventually, Universal agreed to supply movies and shoulder half the cost of the joint venture; the bad news was that, unknown to me, this move did not have the full and wholehearted support of Tom's bosses and eventually we had to buy them out. This was the beginning of a long and often unhappy relationship with Universal.

I looked round for people to run the new company, which we had called Gramercy Pictures. Most of the distribution executives I met were extremely unimpressive and eventually, I settled on a refugee from Miramax Films, Russell Schwartz. In our crowded office in Maple Drive, he soon joined some refugees from Richard Northcott's Nelson Entertainment: Rick Finkelstein, who ran our business affairs, Peter Graves, who advised me on marketing and Deana Elwell, our new Chief Financial Officer.

Anyone setting up a new venture has to reconcile two competing business imperatives: in order to expand one has to build up an organisation (which costs money) and in order to justify such an operation, one needs more product than the organisation can generate in the early years. The balance is very fine.

I decided I was nervous about the limited number of movies I thought we could produce and that genre films seemed too restrictive. Looking round Los Angeles, my attention was caught by Interscope Pictures. Interscope had been founded by Ted Field who came from the famous Marshall Field store family. His No. 2 was a long time Hollywood executive, Robert Cort. They had a deal with Disney and had been responsible, directly or indirectly, for a long list of very commercial, high concept movies in the successful early part of Jeffrey Katzenberg's time as head of Disney Studios. Among them were *Three Men and a Baby* (1987), *Cocktail* (1988) and *The Hand that Rocks the Cradle* (1992). It seemed to me that if we could acquire the product from this entity once its deal with Disney ran out, it would provide that more commercial strand to our movie line up that I was anxious to obtain. Ted had about $30 million tied up in development projects. We took a majority stake in the company in return for paying him back the bulk of his money.

This turned out to be not a great decision. High concept comedies had already peaked and thereafter their success both at Disney and elsewhere began a terminal decline. Secondly, Bob Cort, although unrivalled in his knowledge of the business and in many respects a great producer, was particularly annoying to our other production labels, as he would go on for hours, with great theories as to which movies they should be making, if they wanted any hope of being as successful as he had been. Thirdly, although Ted was generally supportive, he ran Interscope in such a way that it was very difficult for some of the brighter talent there to flourish and soon his attention turned much more to his music concerns, which he also began building up at this time and in which we had no interest. His music company, headed by Jimmy Iovine, turned out to be at the forefront of rap music and the whole new generation of black artists.

But at the time it seemed that an investment in Interscope was a well thought out and important move.

That Christmas, I made the mistake of letting our dour Scottish accountant/Chief Operating Officer, Malcolm Ritchie, organise our Christmas Party. He must have allowed a budget of about US$200 for 30 people and we all squeezed into a tiny room in a cheap Third Street promenade restaurant for our Christmas celebration dinner. The person who looked most at home in these uncongenial surroundings was Jodie Foster.

The mission had begun.

The best of times

In putting together our plan for approval by the Philips Board, our model had conservatively estimated that the first movies we made would be unsuccessful. Boy, were we right in making such an assumption. Among the pretty dreadful films we made and released, either theatrically or for video in 1992 and 1993, were some really dark and unappealing thrillers such as *Kalifornia* with Brad Pitt (Propaganda), *Romeo is Bleeding* with Gary Oldman (Working Title) or over-expensive art films (*Map of the Human Heart*) directed by Vincent Ward (Working Title).

However, we did have a significant success with a black gangster movie called *Posse* staring Mario Van Peebles. This showed that Gramercy, given the right kind of movie, could successfully distribute it in the United States. The only other interesting film of note was an extremely low budget Working Title movie staring and directed by Tim Robbins called *Bob Roberts* which made money and brought a considerable amount of critical acclaim.

Perhaps part of the explanation for this lack of success (apart from the obvious ones such as that we were 'getting our eye in') was the continued concentration and pace of our distribution expansion.

In 1992 we began distributing our movies ourselves in France. We bought an interest in an independent distributor called Pan Europeénne and also gingerly began operations in the UK. Here we distributed our films through Rank, but retained our own marketing group and built up our home video operations.

In the meantime, Manifesto established cornerstone distribution deals with Hoyts in Australia, Senator and Telemunchen Films in Germany, FilmAuro in Italy, Nipon Herald and others in Japan, Nordisk in Scandinavia, Lauren Films in Spain and a host of others.

We also tried, unsuccessfully as it turned out, to integrate the film arm of A&M Records run by Dale Pollock and we also tried, with little success, to set up a Chinese language production and distribution operation in Hong Kong. Also forced on us, were the film operations of the Island Group after its acquisition by PolyGram. Meantime Malcolm Ritchie was busy arranging off-balance sheet financing for our movies, which had two advantages – less use of cash by the Group and, if we had movies that did not work, our quarterly results were smoothed out and losses did not hit the bottom line in as big a way.

In summary, the first two years of our implementation stage combined aggressive expansion of our distribution operations with a singular lack of success with our movies. However, the corner was about to be turned, as in September 1993, we started to test screen a small film made by Working Title called *Four Weddings and a Funeral.*

6
Four Weddings and a Funeral

Richard Curtis is a fabulous writer. He is also notoriously a very nice guy. I first came across him consciously, when Tim Bevan at Working Title showed me the movie that he'd made with him in 1989 called *The Tall Guy*. Before that, he was very famous for his work with Rowan Atkinson on the TV series *Black Adder*.

Courtesy Stephen Morley

RICHARD CURTIS

For whatever reason, *The Tall Guy* was not a commercial hit. However, when Tim Bevan sent Stewart Till and myself the script of *Four Weddings and a Funeral* in 1992, it was one of the most promising scripts we had read. Originally intended to be a production funded by Film Four, the film arm of UK broadcaster Channel 4, it had had a rocky start. Pre-production had been abandoned for creative reasons. It did not take long for Stewart and I to agree that we should back it and we sent it for approval to Alain Lévy on the 18th December 1992. He green lit it (see illustration below) on 23rd December and we thought no more about it until the rough cut came together in 1993. The original budget was US$4.3 million, of which Channel 4 Television in the UK contributed US$1.2 million. In our application for approval, the profit projected was a low of $1m and a high of $2.4m.

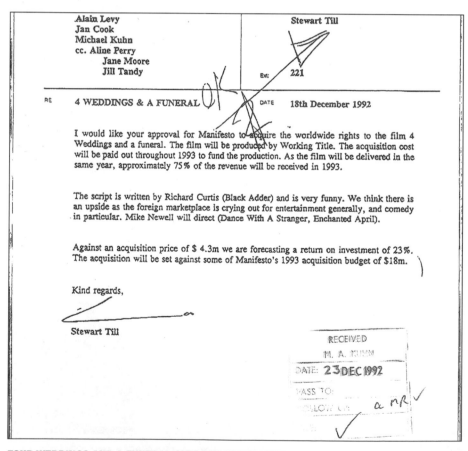

FOUR WEDDINGS AND A FUNERAL GETS THE GREEN LIGHT

In mid year, I attended a screening in London and, although the film was in very rough form, it looked funny and promising. Almost immediately, our American distribution team at Gramercy started a ludicrous argument that the title needed changing as any mention of death in America would be disastrous at the box office. The titles they suggested included: *The Pleasures of Merely Circulating, Loitering in Sacred Places, Skulking Around, Tales of True Love and Near Misses* and *Strays*. Of the last, they rightly remarked: 'This one needs some good copy to set up'. Fortunately, their energy ran out before their ability to find a better title could deliver anything viable and the original title stuck.

On the 22nd September 1993, *Four Weddings* was tested at the Mann Criterion Theatre in Santa Monica, California, before 330 members of the public aged (as the National Research Group Inc reported) 21-54 years of age, 56 per cent females and 44 per cent males, with 44 per cent under 30 and 56 per cent 30 and older. The results were encouraging, but not standout. When the audience filled in forms to show how they rated the movie, 37 per cent thought it was excellent, 38 per cent very good, for a combined score of 75 per cent high favourable, against a norm of 55 per cent. This is considered satisfactory. Those who would definitely recommend it came to 63 per cent of the audience, against the normal 45 per cent. Again satisfactory, but not standout. Hugh Grant came in for the most approval, while the ending was considered predictable and not very exciting.

The team put their heads together. Mike Newell, the director, Tim Bevan, the producers Duncan Kenworthy and Richard Curtis and myself, thought about the fact that the audience who stayed behind after the main screening to discuss the film, kept mentioning that they would like to know what happened to the characters after the film finished. At first this seemed a completely ludicrous issue to try to address as it would require a whole other film to satisfy that demand.

However, after much thought we came up with the idea that it might be possible to add, in the end title sequence, a series of stills, showing weddings of each of the main characters other than the principals, that would indicate what had happened to them all. This was quickly added and a month later on the 14th October the film was screened again, this time on the East Coast of the United States in Secaucus, New Jersey.

Bingo! The National Research Group reported this time that, although this audience liked the movie less than the Santa Monica audience, it was still rated above average, despite the fact that this was a much broader demographic audience. The ending was rated excellent. We decided to finish the movie and began planning the release.

The first decision was whether to go first in the United Kingdom or in the United States. This was not an easy decision, but eventually it was thought that if we failed in the United States we might still succeed in England whereas the opposite was not true. On the other hand, if we succeeded in the United States, the outlook for the UK was very good.

Planning the US release was long drawn-out, nerve wracking and in the end, a triumph. As I wrote to David Aukin, who was then Head of Drama at Channel 4: 'One day I'll tell you what's been involved in bringing this movie to market – had I known what I now know about US theatrical distribution, I would have become Head of Drama for Channel 4 instead!'. The first thing we thought about was giving the film a platform at the Sundance Film Festival in January 1994. In fact, we took two films there, the other was a lovely small film called *Backbeat* about the lost Beatle, Stuart Sutcliffe, directed by Ian Softley and starring Stephen Dorff and Ian Hart. It had been produced by Nik Powell and also involved Channel 4 as an investor.

Four Weddings was invited to open the Sundance Film Festival, which is held in Park City, a small town in the mountains above Salt Lake City, Utah. However, the opening night in those days was held in Salt Lake City itself, to accommodate the local supporters.

While there was no doubt that *Four Weddings* had been extremely well received at the Salt Lake City screening, the Festival screenings of *Backbeat* seemed to us, and many other punters, to have received a much better, even ecstatic, reception.

Nonetheless, the attention garnered for *Four Weddings* at Sundance was high, the word of mouth extremely positive and the feedback encouraged us to proceed with an innovative plan for launching the film in the States.

Now the main problem we faced was this: by the 1990s, most studios had discovered TV advertising of movies. This meant they inevitably got involved in very large TV expenditure, as well as ads in the newspapers and on billboards. In a country the size of the United States, this meant that the P&A (prints and advertising) budget could easily require in the region of US$15-20 million just to open the movie. The risk may be worthwhile if one was confident that it was a broad-appeal movie that could generate box office of $30m or more – because as one only got back 40-50 per cent of the amount paid at the box office, one needed that amount just to recover the P&A expenditure. After that, one hoped to recover the negative cost and make a profit from TV and video revenue.

However, with a little movie that had almost no stars in it other than Andie McDowell, the risk was enormous. None of us felt confident in applying to our bosses for the kind of money that we would need to go head to head with the major studios – particularly in our media spend.

Eventually Peter Graves, our dour but reliably brainy marketing consultant, myself and our marketing team devised a release strategy that has been much copied since. We decided to release on a very small number of screens in New York and Los Angeles and in those two cities we would spend a disproportionately high amount of TV advertising money in order to be competitive. We thereby hoped to get a high per screen average – i.e total box office for the released weekend divided by the number of screens. If this was high enough, it would convince other theatres outside those cities to support our movie and allow us to spend more money on advertising and prints in additional markets and so gradually roll out the movie to a large number of screens over the whole country. I set out these considerations to my boss Alain Lévy in a note of February 24th 1994.

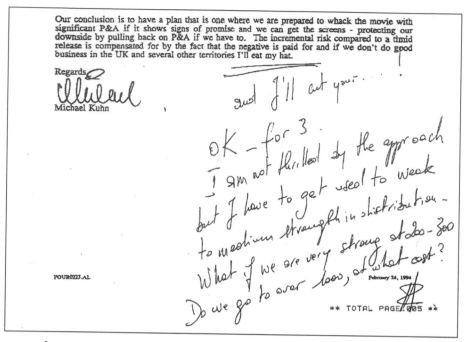

Our conclusion is to have a plan that is one where we are prepared to whack the movie with significant P&A if it shows signs of promise and we can get the screens - protecting our downside by pulling back on P&A if we have to. The incremental risk compared to a timid release is compensated for by the fact that the negative is paid for and if we don't do good business in the UK and several other territories I'll eat my hat.

Regards,

Michael Kuhn

POUR0223.AL

and I'll cut your...

OK – for 3.
I am not thrilled by the approach but I have to get used to weak to medium strength in distribution –
What if we are very strong at 200–300 What if we go to over 1000, at what cost?
Do we go to over 1000,

February 24, 1994

** TOTAL PAGE.005 **

ALAIN LÉVY APPROVES THE P&A SPEND FOR FOUR WEDDINGS

The first option was a wide release – say 1,000 screens released within three weeks of the initial limited opening. The total marketing costs would come to $11.3m. Our problem with this particular strategy was that Gramercy was new as a distributor and its ability to book and hold as many as 1,000 screens from the outset was extremely doubtful. We would need to earn $15m at the box office to breakeven (including contribution from TV and video). The second option was a limited release of under 300 prints. This would still cost $5.5m but there was no way we could achieve results of more than $5-7.5m at the box office. The third option was a limited release widening out. Under this plan we would run the film on four to five screens, broadening the next weekend to approximately 20 to 25 screens in twelve cities and thereafter to 200-300 screens and, if successful, to 700 or 800. I told Alain Lévy that my conclusion was that this plan was one whereby we could 'whack the movie with some significant P&A if it showed signs of promise', protecting downside by pulling back on spending if we have to. I said the incremental risk compared to a timid release would be compensated for by the fact that the negative had been paid for already, out of our international markets and if we didn't do good business in the UK and several other territories, I would eat my hat. Lévy responded that he agreed with my plan, but if it didn't work he would 'not make me eat my hat but cut off my ...'. And so we set to work.

Claudia Gray, our head of PR, began to work the stars extremely hard. Hugh Grant did every interview going. It took some time to realise that he had come forward as the star of the movie. It was so firmly in our mind that Andie McDowell was the star, that when early press reaction indicated that they only wanted to talk to Hugh, we kept pushing Andie forward saying, 'You don't understand, he's not the star of the movie, she is!'. It was an interesting lesson in how not to let the preconceptions formed by considerations that went into producing the movie, cloud the reality of reactions when it comes to marketing the film.

HUGH GRANT

The next task was to develop some excellent TV commercials and trailers, but we never really managed to get together a totally wonderful TV spot. A report on February 15th on one of our trailers showed that the combined definite and probable interest in the movie, based on title and stars before seeing the trailer, was 39 per cent, which rose to 65 per cent after having seen our trailer. This was encouraging, until one looked at the norms, which were 45 per cent rising to 70 per cent.

Rather unusually, in addition to our TV spots, the poster assumed a very great significance in our campaign. Given that we were going to open in only two cities to begin with, we wanted to have a very large outdoor presence. It took a long time to get the poster right and we had to do a special shoot to get the artwork we wanted. The purpose was to show a relationship between our two stars and the striking logo. The end result, although not used in the UK, was perfect for the softer US market and particularly in wintry New York, where we were able to put the image on every bus shelter. It proved most effective in raising awareness.

One of the most important considerations in releasing a movie, is the weekend you choose to open. If you choose well you can sail into open water competitively and do extremely well. If you choose badly, the competitive environment can be so tough, that the available amount of revenues is spread too thinly and an otherwise successful film can sink without much trace. Sitting together with Peter Graves and Russell Schwartz, we spotted a potential gap.

While we had originally anticipated releasing the film in early May, it seemed that our only competition in early April was a movie called *The Paper* which was a comedy directed by Ron Howard staring Michael Keaton, Robert Duval and Glenn Close. Apart from that, the competition was relatively light with movies such as *Guarding Tess* and *Lightning Jack* and *The Ref*, the rest being *Schindler's List* (in its 13th week of release) and *Mrs. Doubtfire* (in its 16th week).

We decided to go on Wednesday 9th March and chose two movie theatres in New York and three in Los Angeles. As it got nearer to the date, we looked anxiously at the 'tracking' reports. These track awareness and definite interest among competing movies that have opened, are opening or are about to open. However, in our case it was only of marginal use because this tracking covered national awareness and interest, whereas we were concentrating on just two cities. Nonetheless, the awareness was growing as was the interest. This was a good sign.

On our opening day, I anxiously awaited the first figures that would come in after the mid-day screenings in New York. As New York was some 3 hours ahead of Los Angeles, this meant that by late morning, these numbers were coming in. To my horror, they seemed unaccountably 'soft'. Having spoken to our New York office, Linda Ditrinco, our representative, told me what had happened. One of the New York theatres was a multiplex. The movie had been put on at its smallest screen and had sold out completely with people unable to get in. By contrast, other movies in the complex which had been playing for some time played in largely empty theatres. I asked why we couldn't change to a bigger theatre. The problem was that big and powerful studios were distributing the other movies and would go nuts at the theatre manager and the circuit if they were taken off the big screen and put on a smaller screen. If we did nothing however, our screen averages would look poor which would be devastating not only for roll out in the US, but consequently for our international plans.

What was to be done? Linda said she had a plan. She did a deal with the theatre manager to swap movies so that we had a big house at the evening show when most of our audience would come. Since the competitor's movie was at the big screen at an earlier show, hopefully no one would find out. Nobody did. On that single initiative hinged much of the subsequent history of *Four Weddings*. Once the switch was made, our average looked great. On five screens we took $18,566. By the time the weekend was finished, this gross had risen to $176,000, with a three day average per screen of $27,697, way ahead of what we had hoped for.

We also undertook some exit surveys of those attending the opening weekend and found that the reality was much better than our pre-release tests might have suggested. In total, 89 per cent thought the movie was either excellent or very good, against the norm of 60 per cent, and 80 per cent said they would definitely recommend the movie, compared to a norm of 50 per cent.

HUGH GRANT   ANDIE MACDOWELL

A MIKE NEWELL FILM

four Weddings and a funeral 1 5

FIVE GOOD REASONS TO STAY SINGLE

PolyGram Filmed Entertainment and Channel Four Films Present a Working Title Production
a Mike Newell Film Hugh Grant Andie McDowell "Four Weddings And A Funeral" Kristin Scott Thomas
Title Credits Title Credits Title Credits Title Credits Title Credits Title Credits & Rowan Atkinson
Casting Director Title Credits US Casting Title Credits Production Designer Maggie Grey Costume Designer Lindy Fleming Editor Jon Gregory
Director of Photography Title Credits Original Music by Title Credits Title Credits Co-Executive Producer Richard Curtis
Executive Producers Title Credits and Title Credits Written by Title Credits Produced by Title Credits Directed by Mike Newell

We obviously had to push on with our plan. Alain Lévy agreed the substantial marketing costs required (three times the movie's cost). We decided to increase the number of prints to 18 on the 17th March and then slowly roll out to 200 and thereafter 600 or more. So it was, that just over a month later, on the weekend of April 15th to 17th 1994, *Four Weddings and a Funeral* reached No. 1 at the US Box Office, with a gross of $4,162,489 and a cumulative box office of just over $14m. Our competition, *The Paper*, released by Universal, grossed just over $3m that weekend and all other competition fell away. The movie went on to gross about $50m in the US on more than 1,000 screens.

By contrast *Backbeat*, for which we had such hopes, made no impact on the US box office. But a significant turning point had been reached. We had built up our own distribution system from nothing and, with our own movie, had reached No. 1 at the US box office. This was the first time a company run from England, or anywhere outside the US, had achieved such a feat – certainly since the Second World War.

Four Weddings was a wonderful movie and is talked about to this day (gaining the largest ever Channel 4 TV audience when it was screened in Britain in November 1995). Mike Newell, Richard Curtis, Duncan Kenworthy, the cast and crew, ably steered by Tim Bevan and Working Title and supported by Channel 4, delivered a magnificent movie. Previous great British movies had not had the benefit of their own marketing and distribution people in charge in the United States and this was the difference.

In July 1994, I was having lunch with Tom Pollock, who in congratulating me on the success of *Four Weddings*, mentioned that he assumed that we would make $100m bottom line profit. I nodded sagely and the conversation moved on. However, when I got back to the office, I immediately asked our numbers people to figure out why it was that Universal came to this conclusion, as on our most optimistic forecast, PolyGram would make $50-60m profit. The answer, when it came, underlined what I had believed from the beginning – that we had our own distribution in only a few countries of the world, whereas Universal Studios had their own distribution everywhere and the profit came from distribution.

Under Stewart Till's guidance, the international plan for releasing the movie began to roll out, beginning in the UK, where the film became the biggest grossing British movie of all time, reaching a box office of £27,763,000 following its release on the 13th May (helped to no small extent by Hugh Grant's then partner – Liz Hurley – attending the première in a Versace dress held together by one safety pin and getting us on all the front pages next morning). It also received a nomination for the best picture in the Academy Awards and Tim Bevan, rightly, prompted us into paying non-contractual bonuses to everybody in the cast and crew. The film ultimately brought in over US$240 million worldwide. Not bad for a US$4 million movie.

There was little time for self congratulation or celebration. The lesson of this experience was clear. We could release movies in America and worldwide. We had to release them ourselves in order to make the profits that would help us take on Hollywood. We had to speed up our expansion into worldwide distribution, even if our product flow was not quite ready, either in quantity, or quality. The advantage I now had was the confidence of colleagues and a change in perception in the industry that would hopefully benefit us during the years ahead.

7
Chasing the lion: PolyGram, MGM and Kirk Kerkorian

If there is one logo that symbolises Hollywood, it is MGM's lion. The history of MGM is the history of Hollywood and its catalogues include some of the greatest movies ever made. From the mid-1980s however, its early glory became tarnished and it suffered many changes of management and ownership.

PolyGram had twice tried to buy into MGM and, after PolyGram was sold to Universal in 1998, some of our libraries were bought by MGM. This is the story of those encounters and of the enigmatic owner of MGM in recent years – Kirk Kerkorian.

The early history of MGM involved the coming together of the United Artists Corporation and MGM. United Artists was formed in 1919 by Charlie Chaplin, Douglas Fairbanks, Mary Pickford and D.W. Griffith, while MGM-Lowe's was formed in 1924 by combining Metro Pictures, Goldwyn Pictures and Louis B Mayer Productions. In 1929, this became Metro-Goldwyn Mayer. MGM/UA Entertainment Co. was formed in 1981, when MGM acquired all of the outstanding stock of United Artists Corporation. Ted Turner bought MGM/UA in March 1986, but almost immediately ran into financial difficulties and had to sell back United Artists to Kirk Kerkorian's Tracinda Corporation, which quickly went public. In August of that year, it acquired a large part of the library and TV production from Turner and began licensing various operations and other assets including trade name logos, leaving TV rights with Ted Turner. In 1986 United Artists changed its name to MGM/UA Communications Company.

Courtesy Associated Press, AP

KIRK KERKORIAN

When I first got to know the company, it owned about 950 titles in the UA library, the right to distribute the MGM RKO archive and pre-1950 Warner Brother libraries in theatrical, non-theatrical and home video channels, as well as having certain international TV rights. Turner had retained the MGM studio lot, which was subsequently sold to Lorimar Pictures, and the residual rights in the MGM RKO and pre-1950 Warner Brother libraries. Even in 1986 the company had over 3,000 films available for home video.

Kirk Kerkorian, 71 years old in 1988, was the son of Armenian immigrants who settled in Fresno, California. His early business success was based on selling World War II surplus aeroplanes, before starting an airline with unscheduled services between Las Vegas and Los Angeles in 1947. This airline – Trans-International Airline Inc. – was sold to Trans-America Corp in 1968 for $107m.

Kirk Kerkorian moved into real estate in Las Vegas, buying and building various hotels and also making hostile tender offers for Western Airlines, MGM and Columbia Pictures, acquiring various share stakes in the process. In 1976, he decided to concentrate on MGM and, between then and 1981, disposed of his other holdings and gained complete control of MGM. Following the sale of MGM and UA to Ted Turner in 1986, he bought back various pieces of both companies, so that by the time I met him, he owned over 80 per cent of MGM/UA through his Trancinda Corporation, which also owned the MGM Grand and various other assets.

In early 1988, when I was planning the early stages of the film operation, it was announced that MGM/UA was indeed for sale. Accompanied by Merrill Lynch, I visited the then Chairman and CEO of MGM/UA, Lee Rich, and Kerkorian's representative, Steve Silbert. I was told that the asking price was US$30 per share. Merrill Lynch felt that Kerkorian would reject any offer for less than US$20 per share. Prior to the sale announcement, the shares had been trading at US$5.

The bank had sent a team to London who produced their analysis for my colleagues and we decided not to proceed further. However, we let it be known that we might be interested in acquiring MGM/UA's non-USA catalogue, if assured of a continuing flow of products from MGM/ UA.

Somewhat surprisingly, in August, Kerkorian called on David Fine in London. David told him we were not interested in being in the movie business in North America at that time, but may be interested in non-USA rights. He asked me (then based in Los Angeles) to continue discussions.

I proposed to him a joint venture non-USA company owned 50-50 by MGM/UA and PolyGram which would licence the MGM/UA catalogue and new products to PolyGram on a long-term basis. This was rejected and Kerkorian made a counter-proposal, which seemed extremely interesting. On the 18th August 1988, I wrote to Kerkorian summarising his proposal. In essence, there would be a one for one rights issue, which effectively Kerkorian would underwrite, owning as he did, 82 per cent of the 50 million shares in the company, with the public owning 18 per cent. He would then sell to us 50 per cent of the new shares with a price cap of about US$12-13 per share. We would end up with about 22.5 per cent of the company, but, more importantly, we would get exclusive distribution rights for the catalogue and any new productions for home video outside the United States for as long as we were shareholders. We would also acquire the right to distribute the TV catalogue and new productions and to have representation on the Board of UIP.

This meant that the net cost to us of our shares would be about US$9-10. In a company that would be capitalised to produce a serious flow of movies, it seemed to me (insofar as these things can ever be characterised as such) a 'no-brainer'.

I waited for our PolyGram annual convention in Southern Spain that year, hoping to get a positive response from my colleagues.

One Sunday, I was asleep in my small apartment in West Hollywood, when the phone went early in the morning. A voice said 'Hi, Mike'. 'Who's that?' I asked. 'It's Kirk'. Rubbing sleep out of my eyes, I just managed to avoid saying 'Kirk who?' before continuing. Kerkorian asked me to come to his lady friend's house, as he urgently wanted to discuss something with me. His companion at the time was Cary Grant's widow, Barbara Grant. I climbed into my small Mustang convertible rental car and zipped up the road to Bel Air. I got hopelessly lost and ended up on Mulholland Drive at the top of the Hollywood Hills. Calling on my cell phone which would only work from the top of the hills but not in the canyons, the phone was answered by Barbara Grant, who, in the most English way and with the most detailed English style, gave me directions ('Go down the canyon until you see a dreadful house on the right, painted pink; there is a wonderful magnolia tree on the left and after that, count three turnings before turning left...').

Hot, sweaty and embarrassed at my lateness, I arrived at her house. She told me not to worry, the house was difficult to find and I should just take a deep breath and everything would be fine. Kerkorian, after an enthusiastic welcome, explained the reason he wanted a meeting. It turned out that he had been thinking about studio management and come to the conclusion that once PolyGram (or Philips as he insisted on calling it) was on board he would have a blue chip partner so that we could attract 'A' class management. If possible, he would like to replicate the team management that, for example, Disney had with Frank Wells, Michael Eisner and Jeffrey Katzenberg. In fact, he had waiting in the next room one of the potential team who he was really keen on.

This was obviously a set up. We hadn't agreed to buy into MGM/UA. I had no authority to agree to anything. However, now it was too late to avoid being shoved into a room with a potential manager of the studio, who would look on my presence as evidence that a blue chip player such as PolyGram, was going to take an interest in MGM and secure some stability.

Without further ado, I was ushered into a room, where the man and his lawyer were waiting. The choice was indeed surprising. Sitting in front of me was Brandon Tartikoff, the then head of NBC, one of the most successful US TV networks at the time. After a few minutes of me being introduced as the Head of Philips, Tartikoff, looking somewhat surprised, his lawyer looking puzzled, Kerkorian left to get us some coffee and croissants. In the few minutes he was out of the room, Tartikoff asked me what on earth this was all about. I could honestly say I had no idea, other than my theory which I explained to him. Kerkorian returned with the coffee and croissants and we had a cheerful ten minute conversation, whereupon Tartikoff left with his lawyer and Kerkorian seemed extremely pleased with the way the meeting had gone, much to my consternation. My alarm however was not yet over. The phone went, Kirk said, 'Hang on Steve, I'd like my friend Mike to hear this and let us know what he thinks…'. Steve, who I took to be Kerkorian's lawyer, obviously demurred. Kirk said, 'I have no secrets from my friend Mike'. He then put the phone on speaker. The lawyer still hesitated. Kerkorian told him to get on with it. The reluctant lawyer then said that Alan Ladd, who had been running the studio, had offered to resign. Kirk turned to me, 'Mike do you think we should accept it?'. As I had only met Alan Ladd when we had done our deal for *PI*, I knew nothing about him and had no position to opine one way or another. I felt myself truly painted into a corner. Hopping from one leg to the other, I hoped that I was as non-committal as possible. Kirk said 'Okay, I agree with Mike, we should accept his resignation'.

I left the meeting a shaken man.

A few days later, almost a repeat of this meeting took place, this time at Kerkorian's cramped small offices in Beverley Hills. As small talk, I noted a Western genre painting of a cowboy chasing an Indian squaw on his wall. He said it had been a gift and it had an interesting aspect to it that I wouldn't have noticed. He fumbled in his drawer, found a key, inserted it in a small keyhole in the frame of the picture, turned it and opened out the painting to show another canvas behind of the cowboy and the captured squaw.

I was then ushered into a side office to meet the person whom Kerkorian thought would make an excellent partner to run the studio with Brandon Tartikoff. I felt I couldn't be surprised anymore. I was. I went into the meeting room to find Peter Guber sitting there, the same Peter Guber, who had run PolyGram Pictures in the past. Again Kerkorian said he would go and get some sandwiches for lunch. In his case he really meant **go** and went to get sandwiches from a deli down the street. I told the puzzled Guber that it was hard to believe, but it looked as if Kerkorian wanted him and Tartikoff to run MGM together. Guber, who was pretty used to the bizarre, looked stunned. By that time I had decided to go with the flow and pretended that such discussions were an everyday thing for me. We ate the sandwiches and left.

David Fine, never a fan of our film operations, could not be convinced to go ahead with this deal. I felt he was wrong. I felt then, and I still feel, that we could have bought our way into MGM at an extremely reasonable price with little downside risk and avoided all the hassle of having to start a studio from scratch. At the time we could well afford it and such a catalogue would have prepared us heartily for the video bonanza that was to continue throughout the 90s and, as DVD took off, into the 21st Century. However, timing is all and, with MGM, we never had the timing quite right.

My impression was that Kirk Kerkorian, who had been the subject of a blistering article in September 1988 in the magazine *Manhattan Inc*, was very hurt by the perception that he had asset stripped MGM. His own view (which of course had to be taken with a due degree of scepticism) was that he had continually put his hand in his pocket to fund the company and its production slate and had never interfered in it. He felt he had been betrayed by successive managements, who had produced inferior movies, while living high and closing detrimental deals without his knowledge (such as the one whereby the rival Warners had the distribution rights of the UA film library until the end of 1991). There was an element of truth to his perception, but I always felt there were two competing forces within him – one compelling him to execute ever more stunning deals using his asset base and, second, a loyalty to MGM as an institution. To me personally, he was always charming and gracious.

In the next eight years, much happened to MGM as Kerkorian sought to find a partner or buyer after some demeaning sales to rogue Australians and Italians. The French bank, Credit Lyonnais was left owning the company which was completely out of control by this point. Several billion dollars in the hole, Credit Lyonnais decided to put MGM on the market in 1996 and I decided to have another go at buying it. On the 26th March, we began work on the proposal for the PolyGram and Philips' board. The opportunity was extremely exciting; PolyGram had by now a product flow of increasingly attractive films to feed into a studio. MGM lacked films. PolyGram had a very strong international marketing and distribution operation, whereas MGM was the poor relation in the joint venture with Paramount and Universal called UIP which was itself only a joint venture for theatrical release purposes. Universal and Paramount were partners together in another venture called CIC and, while PolyGram had strong international video operations and TV operations, MGM was relatively weak. MGM had a wonderful library compared to PolyGram. In one leap, the acquisition of MGM would have put PolyGram at the forefront of the major studio operations. When we ran the numbers, it was clear that we could make a bid of up to US$2 billion and thereby add $230 million in profit before interest and tax in the first year after a deal, rising to nearly $500 million in profit before interest and tax in the third and subsequent years.

First, however, I was in for a shock. Having done the necessary preparatory work, my team were ready to present the proposal for buying MGM to the PolyGram board and then the Philips board. The PolyGram board at the time was chaired by the former president of PolyGram, David Fine. Immediately before the meeting at which we intended to make our proposal, Jan Timmer, the Chairman of Philips, had appointed Cor Boonstra to take over as chairman of the PolyGram board, but still retaining David Fine on the board. Boonstra, who was subsequently to take over from Jan Timmer, had only recently joined Philips and had little knowledge of PolyGram.

I received a phone call from David Fine saying that there had been a PolyGram board meeting at Gatwick Airport and it had been decided not to go ahead with the bid for MGM. This was quite an amazing development. I had never been in a company or known of a company where board decisions were taken on matters raised by senior management without a management presentation having been made. After discussing the matter with Alan Lévy, I rang back David Fine at Gatwick Airport and insisted on speaking to Boonstra. I told him that I thought this method of approach was extremely ill advised and while it was within the discretion of the PolyGram board to turn down proposals, as a public company, I did not think they could do so responsibly without having heard from me.

Boonstra agreed to hold off a decision until it had been properly considered by a board of both PolyGram and Philips. After this I felt somewhat better, as I knew that Jan Timmer would support us and help pilot the thing through the relevant boards.

And so it was, that the management team, led by Alan Lévy, myself, Jan and Roger Ames, left in mid June of 1996 on the PolyGram jet to meet the relevant boards in Eindhoven. We arrived once again at the stark Philips Headquarters building and waited. And waited. And waited. Roger Ames wandered around the offices pretending to steal what he could from Philips' collection of ornaments as retribution. Alan Lévy fumed. I worried. What we did not know was that the delay had been apparently caused by a major row between Jan Timmer and Cor Boonstra on matters relating to the management of Philips. Eventually we were shown into the gloomy boardroom familiar to me from previous encounters with the Philips board and made our presentation. There were few questions, we were tired and when we came back we were given the go ahead, provided that the amount we paid did not exceed a figure which was approximately US$200 million less than we had recommended.

Nonetheless, we set off to see Lazards, the bankers in New York. On entering the meeting, I found that the principal banker with whom we had been dealing was not there. I knew the game was up and someone else had got in ahead of us. Who was this someone?

Of course it was none other than Kirk Kerkorian who had backed Frank Mancuso, the then chairman of MGM, in his bid to buy the company. Quite apart from the price difference, Kerkorian was in a position to buy the company without worrying about warranties and indemnities and such like. It was a terrible disappointment and gave further fuel to the belief we had within PolyGram management, that the quick moving risk taking style required to be successful in the entertainment business, was inimical to the ethos of a hardware company like Philips, with their ponderous committee-driven ways.

My final encounter with Kerkorian was in 1998, when PolyGram Films itself was for sale. Jerry Perenchio had invited me to meet Kerkorian at Jerry's house in Malibu. I drove over there on a sunny Sunday morning to be greeted by Kerkorian with the words, 'It will be great when I buy PolyGram Films and we merge it with MGM... it will be a great company!'. I took Jerry out into the blinding sun on the balcony overlooking the Pacific and, as usual in my dealings with Kirk, asked him what on earth was going on and what Kerkorian might have meant. Jerry said he had no idea but to listen to him, allow a decent space of time and then go home. Kerkorian asked me to put on paper my ideas on how PolyGram and MGM could fit together. I agreed to do so and that was the last I ever heard from him.

The coda to this long flirtation with the lion was that in 1999 much of PolyGram Film's catalogue was sold to, whom else, but – MGM!

Kerkorian is indeed a mystery wrapped up in an enigma. Well into his 80s, he has the physique of someone less than half his age, the cunning of a master entrepreneur and, beneath it all, unless I am mistaken, a need to correct what in his view was an unjustified image as the biggest asset stripper in Hollywood history. I am sure he has at least a decade of active business life left to see whether this assessment is correct.

8
Green lighting and marketing

Who decides?

From the end of 1993 I got on with the business of consolidating the organisation and 'getting my eye in' on green lighting films.

It had always seemed to me that the studio method of deciding which films to make was extremely flawed. In Hollywood, everything is centralised as much as possible and the head of the studio jealously guards the power to decide which movies to make. If one considers the fact that for every movie that is made, there are four or five contending scripts selected from thousands that are submitted weekly, it will be obvious that the burden of reading on any one person will soon become intolerable and, even if they are assiduous in considering projects, they will soon get burned out.

The consequence of this is that many studios are led from time to time by characters who have been much caricatured in literature and film over the years. Can the project be described in terms of other projects? If you can present something in a shorthand way, it makes it much easier for a studio head to digest. For example, 'This movie is *Notting Hill* meets *Gladiator*'. It leads to management by headline and lack of original thought. Alternatively, projects are pitched according to who they star and who is directing. 'You should make this movie because it's Spike Jonze directing Bruce Willis and it only costs $40 million'. All studios, however, tend to rely on certain producers: 'Never mind the story or who's in it or who's directing it, it's being produced by Jerry Bruckheimer', or if the project follows in the wake of a very successful and often unexpected hit: 'This is the new *Full Monty*' or 'This is the new *Scream*'.

The rather depressing statistic is that it doesn't really matter who's running a studio. If you make 15 to 20 Hollywood size movies a year and market them professionally on a world-wide basis, you will have enough hits irrespective of who's in charge. To justify to some degree this blanket investment every year, the historic record is that there will be a very big hit every three years and a *Titanic* or similar every five years.

Having thought about this process, I came to the conclusion that there were two issues I had to address when a movie came forward for green lighting. (It should be borne in mind that I tried wherever possible to ensure that no movies ever came directly to me but only through one of our trusted labels.) First of all, one had to be aware of what the numbers looked like. On a medium case scenario, would projected income exceed projected expenses by a sufficiently large margin to make the project worthwhile? As important, two further secondary questions arose: if the movie was a complete turkey, would the loss wipe out the whole film division? If the movie was a bit hit would the profit be sufficient to help pay for the inevitable predominant number of unsuccessful movies on that year's slate? Secondly what did our marketing people think about the project, the cast, the director and other elements?

I always had to explain to the organisation, that it was not a question of bean-counters and marketing men deciding which movies to make. That would be extremely foolish. However, it would be even more foolish to decide which movies to make without taking note of what the numbers looked like, or what the marketing people felt about it. To this end, we developed what we called the control sheet (see Chapter 15). From a very early stage in the development of a project, a label would start putting together a control sheet. In order to do so, they had to get projections from our international sales operation, from our international territories and from our American distribution operation. This led to a healthy tension. If our marketing distribution and bean counting people were too harsh in their judgements, no movies would get green lit, there would be no product flow and we would all be out of a job. If they were not rigorous enough, they knew they would have to pick up an awful film and spend months trying to get it to market and achieve some revenues. There were frequent rows between the labels and the marketing and distribution people, but slowly the control sheet, with a good deal of compromise, would come together, so that often, by the time the movie came to be green lit, there was little by way of decision that had to be made. The movies sort of green lit themselves.

I also found that, as a result of this process, the development people were not developing movies in a vacuum; they were very aware from the beginning of what the marketing group felt about certain types of projects, certain casts, certain genres and developed their movies accordingly. One of the problems in the United Kingdom has been that, in the absence of a strong studio, projects are often developed in isolation from market realities and the result has been a very disappointing level of success for scripts developed independently in the UK.

Furthermore, once a film was in production, it was a salutary reminder to carry round (as I did) a summary of the control sheets for all the movies we had, to show what our expectations were when it was approved compared to current performance.

This system, I felt at the time and feel now, is infinitely superior to the green lighting system at the major Hollywood studios. It was always very clear at PolyGram who was responsible, whether for good or ill, for producing a movie. If Tim Bevan and Eric Fellner made a movie such as *Four Weddings*, they should get the credit. If on the other hand they made a movie that was less successful such as *Chicago Joe and the Showgirl* they should take the blame. Creative decision making was at a level much closer to the writing and directing talent and the financial and marketing consequences were discussed more collectively, each interested group feeling committed to the other.

Just as I felt the label system and the green lighting system I have described worked well, so too I thought that the studio system internationally was not as good as that which we developed.

Being John Malkovich

Of all the movies I green lit, the one directors are most interested in hearing about is *Being John Malkovich* (1999).

Much as I would like to claim credit for my perspicacity in approving production of this movie, I have to admit, in all honesty, that I did everything I could do to prevent it being made. I forget whether it was pitched to me by the Propaganda producer, my friend Steve Golin, or whether the pitch included the director Spike Jonze and/or the writer Charlie Kaufman.

In any event the pitch went something like this:

'This is about a young guy who is an unemployed puppeteer. His wife is nuts, likes monkeys and is also unemployed. The hero gets a job as a filing clerk in an office that is only half a floor high. He finds a hole in the wall, which leads to John Malkovich's head. He then exits on the Jersey turnpike.'

I seriously thought they were pulling my leg. They told me they weren't. I asked if John Malkovich was attached. They said no. This seemed a good way out and instead of telling Steve to push off and never come back, I told him to push off and never come back until we had John Malkovich. Several months later he came back and said they had got John Malkovich to do the movie. I asked how much the movie would cost. They said US$15 million. I said that was far too expensive and it had to be under US$10 million. Some more months passed and sure enough the budget was reduced to under $10 million. I told them that I thought the cast needed to be bigger than just John Malkovich. They went away and came back a few months later having cast John Cusack, Cameron Diaz and Catherine Keener.

I ran some numbers.

It seemed to me it was very difficult to lose any money on this project given that it could probably be financed almost entirely from international sales. However, Steve Golin knew me too well and knew he needed a clincher.

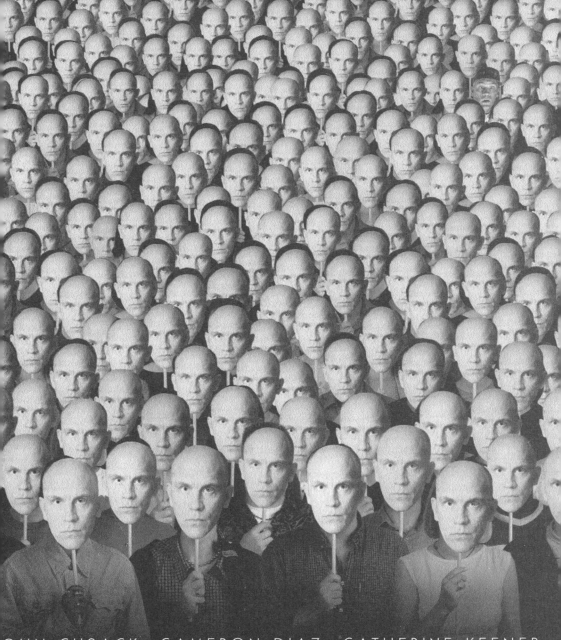

JOHN CUSACK   CAMERON DIAZ   CATHERINE KEENER

BEING JOHN MALKOVICH

A FILM DIRECTED BY SPIKE JONZE

UNIVERSAL PICTURES INTERNATIONAL Presents A PROPAGANDA FILMS/SINGLE CELL PICTURES Production JOHN CUSACK CAMERON DIAZ CATHE RINE KEENER ORSON BEAN "BEING JOHN MALKOVICH"
NY KAY PLACE and JOHN MALKOVICH Music by CARTER BURWELL Editor ERIC ZUMBRUNNEN Production Designer K.K. BARRETT Director of Photography LANCE ACORD Executive Producers CHARLIE KAUFMAN MICHAEL KUHN
Produced by MICHAEL STIPE and SANDY STERN STEVE GOLIN VINCENT LANDAY Written by CHARLIE KAUFMAN Directed by SPIKE JONZE

UNIVERSAL

 www.beingjohnmalkovich.com

VER WANTED TO BE SOMEONE ELSE?

I had planned (quite separately) an artists' retreat to a wonderful place in the middle of Mexico over one weekend. He got Spike Jonze and his then girlfriend, Sophie Coppola invited. We had a riotous time. The party included Joel Coen, Alan Parker, Michael Apted and many other fun people. Somewhere amongst the Margharitas, I intimated to Steve Golin that we would do the movie. He held me to it.

Filming was underway. I attended the Toronto Film Festival and there was an airline strike, which meant that someone had to hire a jet to get stars in and out of Toronto and I hitched a lift on board one of the jets going back to Los Angeles. On board was Cameron Diaz. During the course of the trip she discovered that I was putting up the money for *Being John Malkovich*, which she was returning to Los Angeles to film. She broke up in laughter at the thought that anyone would finance this film that she had agreed to do. It did not inspire confidence in me.

The film turned out to be a work of considerable genius and profit. If I were a wiser man, I would have resisted telling this story.

International distribution

Typically, outside the United States, studios tend to divide responsibility for exploiting their films, into divisions linked to the type of exploitation, rather than the country of exploitation. So, for example, if a film is distributed throughout Europe in the movie theatres, the head of the theatrical exploitation division back in Hollywood is in charge of that revenue stream. Video reports in to the head of video and TV in to the head of TV. They all have their own overheads, presidents, vice presidents and differing financial objectives. The head of the National Organisation in France or Germany, Japan or Australia is more a co-ordinator, greatly subservient to the relevant divisions. This has two consequences: firstly, there is the build-up of a very large overhead and cost structure which diminishes the returns to the studio and leads the corporate group and Wall Street to believe that the movie business is less profitable than it might be. Secondly, marketing is led out of Hollywood with little or no regard to national considerations.

At PolyGram, we felt that within very broad limits, the country should be king. If you didn't have a good performance on a slate of films from a particular national organisation, you had the wrong guy running it and should change it. And so it was we were able to attract a particularly talented team of people to each of our national organisations. No executive worth his salt in France or Germany, Japan or Australia would want to work in an organisation where they had almost no autonomy and had to report to some guy in Hollywood. On the other hand, at PolyGram, they were really in charge of almost everything that happened in the exploitation of films in their territory, whether on video, on TV or in the movie theatre. We made major moves in building these national organisations in almost every year between 1993 and 1998. In order, they were: France, Benelux, the UK, Spain, Canada, Australia, Germany and Italy.

When Stewart Till and I decided whether or not to open up a distribution territory, there were usually two reasons prodding us. Firstly, it had become difficult to sell movies to third parties in that country for whatever reason and, secondly, if there were conditions available by which we could set up distribution. How it was done varied. For example, in Benelux we bought a company called Movie Film Productions, which was an independent company to which we had historically sold our films and, in that case, they wanted to be bought. In other countries like Australia, there was a very strong executive, in that case Richard Sheffield, who was available and looking for a job. In Spain, we had an arrangement with the Spanish organisation, Sogepaq and in the UK we originally had our own marketing group, but used Rank to physically distribute the movies, although in the end took over the distribution function as well.

These strong national organisations, under the management of Stewart Till, were forceful in their views about the movies we made and how they should be marketed and, by and large, this was to good effect. In due course, we also became an important centre of acquisition, as our distribution organisations could handle more product than we could actually produce. For example, our UK organisation successfully acquired *Twelve Monkeys*. At the end, probably 75 per cent of what we distributed world-wide was self produced, 25 per cent was acquired and 5 per cent were local language films or acquisitions just for a particular territory.

The relationship with PolyGram's international music operation was very helpful in the early days of setting up an organisation; we didn't have to get local expertise on offices, tax, accounting, politics and other local matters. As we grew in size and importance, it often became the case that the film operations had, of necessity, to separate themselves from the record company and that led to a good deal of argument about how much was charged in infrastructure costs to the film operation.

While managing these international operations was complex, the case for growing our international distribution organisations was straight-forward and not high profile within the boardroom of PolyGram. When it came to opening up our own distribution in the United States, that was a different matter.

The decision to move into distributing our bigger budget movies as well as our smaller films was very difficult. On the one hand, unless and until we became responsible for 'dressing our own shop window' in the United States by being in charge, in all respects, of marketing and distribution, we would not be considered a first rank player by the Hollywood community. On the other hand, to give up the safety cushion of having sold the rights to someone else for the US for anywhere between 35 and 50 per cent of the budget and on top of that having to come up with the marketing expenditure to distribute our big movies was enough to make the bravest proponent of US distribution pause.

Uninformed people often thought that the biggest risk in setting up US distribution in movies is the cost of hiring a distribution organisation. It is not. It is being 'on the hook' for the American share of the negative cost and the prints and advertising risk.

After endless modelling discussion and agonising, we eventually opened up our full distribution structure on 2nd May 1997. I had hired a veteran of the business, Andrew Fogelson, to run it together with Peter Graves, whom I had known for many years as a marketing consultant. The first movie we distributed was *The Game* starring Michael Douglas and directed by David Fincher. It did not do huge business, but showed that we could open a major movie with a major star and be competitive with any other Hollywood studio. Personally, the moment we were up and running with US distribution, I felt a sea change in the attitude of American talent to PolyGram. Suddenly, we had arrived.

This was the fulfilment of a dream for me; never before had a European based studio had its own US distribution as well as distribution in all major territories of the world. Now, we could take on a purely British project such as *Bean* and, by focussing all our efforts, make it into a world-wide success. We were not reliant on whether Miramax liked one of our films and were willing to put their considerable talents and money to work to make it a success. We were in charge of our own destiny. We could access world-wide profit margins. We had the ability to 'make the numbers work' in the film business. In addition, I felt that particularly in our film selection procedure and our international marketing, we were better in many respects than the Hollywood studios and more talent friendly.

Also we were becoming more experienced in choosing which projects to back.

When I walked out of the door of PolyGram for the last time, I left behind films such as *Notting Hill* (world-wide box office over US$240 million), a half share in *The Green Mile*, the hit sci-fi movie *Pitch Black*, the hit low budget movie *Being John Malkovich*, as well as a development slate that included *Nurse Betty, Captain Correlli's Mandolin* and *Bridget Jones' Diary*.

As I look back over the movies that we brought out in the last few years of PolyGram, I like to think we were developing a slate that was a good mixture of big commercial world-wide hits, such as *Bean* and *Notting Hill*, with movies that both did well and received great critical acclaim such as *Fargo, Elizabeth, The Usual Suspects* and *The Borrowers*, as well as those that may not have been so successful commercially, but of which I was proud, such as *The Big Lebowski, Return to Paradise, The Game*, and *Nell*. We had made some very good films in languages other than English, such as *Le Huitieme Jour* and *Le Ridicule*. We had had big successes with unlikely features such as the Oscar winning documentary *When We Were Kings*. We had had a go at making market-driven films; sometimes with no success, *Barb Wire* (starring Pamela Anderson) and sometimes with great success, *Spice World*. We picked up and successfully marketed the work of innovative film-makers who had put their own movies together (*Lock Stock and Two Smoking Barrels*) and altogether won some 14 Oscars.

Courtesy 20th Century Fox

JODIE FOSTER, NATASHA RICHARDSON, LIAM NEESON

As I look at the numbers, I see that in 1999, given the organisation we had and the product coming through it, we would have been in profit about one year later than had been projected in our original 1991 presentation to Philips.

All in all I considered this not bad going in eight years.

9
The end

'PolyGram Up for Grabs' was the headline in Daily Variety on Thursday May 7th 1998. May 7th was also my 49th birthday.

The previous day, Philips had announced that 'it is evaluating various strategic options with respect to its stake in PolyGram'.

Towards the end of 1997, my colleagues and I on the board of PolyGram had come to the conclusion that Philips was losing its interest in being an owner of our company. We tried to get them more involved by hosting a seminar in New York, where we took them through all the economics of the music business in general and PolyGram in particular and sought to get them familiar and easy with the business. It was clear there was little interest in putting in the effort to become knowledgeable and involved in the company. There was no chance that the head of Philips was going to turn into a Jack Welch – that is to say an executive in charge of a conglomerate, who could one day be involved and make decisions on matters to do with investment banking, the next with industrial company matters, the next with the running of NBC or other entertainment interests.

Our bosses were interested in one thing and one thing only – the various businesses of the hardware company Philips. History meant little to them. The possible benefits of a hardware/software venture meant even less. The will to grow PolyGram into a world-wide leader among media groups was not in their blood.

Cor Boonstra in particular gave the impression that he was nervous about Philips' investment in PolyGram. We guessed that he was nervous in not knowing the entertainment business and having to rely on mercurial and difficult management such as Alain Lévy; he was nervous about the threat posed to the music business and PolyGram by the internet; he was nervous at the venture into the film business; he was nervous that if he wanted to sell there wouldn't be many buyers; and he was nervous that his ambitions for the growth in the share price of Philips might be adversely affected.

We decided to have it out. We convened a meeting in a country house hotel, south of London. Alain Lévy, Jan Cook, the CFO at PolyGram, Roger Ames and myself met up with Cor Boonstra and his financial people. After a pleasant dinner we set out to discover the truth. We said that we thought that he was not particularly interested in PolyGram as such. He said that was correct. We then discussed whether he would like Philips to get out of their investment if they could. He said he would. We then devised a plan whereby we would each explore various exit scenarios with Philips and reconvene in due course. He agreed with this plan.

We headed back to London glad that the issue was now clear and we were anxious to make progress on finding an exit route for Philips. It was a complex matter because PolyGram was held at a very insignificant amount on the balance sheet of Philips and any sale would trigger large tax problems.

How naive we seemed in retrospect! While we worried about Philips' tax bill, Cor Boonstra, together with his bankers, had already started negotiations behind our backs with Seagram, who themselves had just terminated acquisition talks with EMI. When Alain Lévy went to see Seagram to discuss possible merger plans, he did not know and was not told of the Philips/Seagram discussions. This was perceived by Alain as betrayal on a grand scale by Boonstra. It certainly was not the most honourable way of proceeding. The only explanation was that Boonstra felt he could not trust Lévy or his team.

Our naivety, in assuming that Philips would deal honourably with the management of PolyGram, was bolstered by our disbelief that Philips would totally ignore the possibility of leveraging their investment in PolyGram into a large alliance that would assist them in their consumer electronics and chip businesses. For example (and ironically), there may have been the possibility of an alliance with Vivendi which would have created a European super-group with music, broadcast and film interests from whom Philips could have benefited substantially, while going forward in their core businesses. That was not to be and so it was that a shocked Alain Lévy told me what he had just been told, immediately prior to the announcement by Philips, that we were for sale and a deal had more or less been done with Seagram.

As a public company, we had to take independent advice. We hired one of the foremost New York take-over attorneys (Marty Lipton) who told us bluntly that as Philips owned PolyGram with a minority public float, they could do what they liked with the company. There was a Dutch procedural law in our favour that would allow us to leverage a few concessions out of Seagram and Philips, but that was all. What did we want? We told him to try and get preservation of rights for PolyGram employees, non-discrimination against them and the right to have a chance to sell PolyGram Filmed Entertainment as a going concern.

After much to-ing and fro-ing, a late night meeting in New York between Edgar Bronfman, Alain Lévy, Cor Boonstra and their various advisers signed off on this deal and the Seagram deal was announced. They were to buy PolyGram from Philips in a transaction which valued PolyGram at $10.6 billion. About $2 billion was paid for in Seagram stock and the rest in cash.

On the 21st May I wrote to my PFE colleagues telling them of the sale and our opportunity to try to sell PFE to a third party. I told them that a divestiture committee would be formed of myself, a Philips representative and a Seagram representative. Goldman Sachs would act jointly for the divestiture committee. Societe Generale Bannon would act for PolyGram.

In retrospect two things stopped us having a successful sale of PFE; firstly, by having to accept the Seagram investment bankers as the bankers for the divestiture committee, I had no control of the process. Secondly, the politics and jockeying for position within the management of Seagram would prove to be difficult for me to handle, in that potential bidders could not get quick and reasonable answers to their offers. Nonetheless, we put together a sales presentation and saw among others EMI, Carlton and Canal Plus.

The asset we had was attractive. We had a strong slate of movies in the can (including *Notting Hill*). We had a strong development slate. We could produce up to 16 mainstream Hollywood movies per year. We controlled access directly to distribution of movies in 14 countries, representing approximately 85 per cent of the global entertainment market. We had strong media distribution capabilities for film and television products. We owned the third largest post-1948 film catalogue in the world, with approximately 1,500 feature films and 10,000 hours of television programming. Our film library was projected to generate approximately $314 million in aggregate free cash flow through 2002. We had earnings before interest, tax, depreciation and amortisation of $269 million on revenues of over $2 billion projected for that same year.

We had in place an off-balance sheet non-recourse film funding facility of some $600 million, which would take care of all our production financing needs, without the need of further funding from any buyer.

So what was the problem? I felt that had I had bankers acting directly for me and had I been able to communicate directly with the decision makers at Seagram, we could have sold the company to Canal Plus. However, it was not to be and for whatever reason, Canal Plus in particular was put off and left the scene and EMI, who came very close to making a bid, withdrew at the last minute.

I left my office in Los Angeles at the beginning of December 1998. Universal Pictures' President and COO, Chris McGurk, who was the beneficiary of PolyGram not being sold off as a whole, since he would now be responsible for the integration of PolyGram into Universal and presumably be in charge of the international operations of Universal, almost immediately left to take a job as co-head of MGM. With him gone, there was no reason to stop the overall break-up of PFE, the sale of its catalogue to help the cash position of Seagram and a dispersal of its management into other companies world-wide.

Stewart Till stayed on for about a year hoping to make PolyGram's international operations the core of Universal's future international operations in place of UIP. This was not to happen either and he left at the end of 1999.

At the time of beginning to write this book (December 2000) Jean Luc Messier, the Chairman of Vivendi, triumphantly steered through his shareholders the acquisition of the Seagram Group, including Universal and what was left of PFE. Philips voted their shares in favour.

People often ask me how I felt about the fact that we were never allowed to reach our final destination, which was so close. Curiously, the sudden end of both PolyGram and its film operations did not really affect me emotionally. On analysis, I think this was because, when we put together our presentation of PolyGram Films to potential buyers, it became clear to me that our destination had been reached. We would turn profitable in 1999 and, given no greater level of success in future years than in the past, we would have caught up all past losses and be in aggregate profit by the year 2001 – the year in which my current contract expired. In a sense, the balance of three years on my contract would have been a period of consolidation and simply keeping a light hand on the tiller until we reached dockside. Much less interesting, challenging and exciting than the years of building the group.

As to the disposal overall of PolyGram, it was and is a time of consolidation in the business world. Subsequent events showed that even a company as big as Seagram was likely to be acquired and who knows what may happen to Vivendi in the years ahead. One cannot allow oneself to become over emotional about such matters. To have worked for one company for 23 years and to have been given the opportunities I had is not an experience likely to be repeated for future generations – in that respect, executive life is becoming harder and the fun less.

And so as I packed up my household and family to set off back to life in England, the impact on me personally was much less than one might have been led to expect. I was ready for pastures new and felt that much had been achieved. As I was packing up to leave Los Angeles, a lovely surprise, Stephen Woolley, the well known producer of such films as *The Crying Game* telephoned me, to ask if I would agree to accept an award, from the British Academy of Film and Television Arts, for outstanding contribution to film. I don't know whether he expected me to say no, but I agreed and at a ceremony in May 1999 I was given the Michael Balcon Award and the BBC had prepared a wonderful video featuring tributes from Robert Redford, Jodie Foster, Michael Douglas and others. In my acceptance speech, I did and said what was expected on such an occasion – in particular referring to the thousands of employees of PolyGram Films who had really been responsible for our great adventure. The only note of sadness was that we still have no London-based film studio to compete with Hollywood. I still have the ambition one day to put that right.

PART TWO

Influences, titans and characters

10
Arthur Krim

I never met Arthur Krim. He transformed the moribund United Artists into the dominant studio in Hollywood. His business philosophy was perhaps the most influential on my own thinking about the way to structure a film studio.

Like me, he had started as a lawyer (although much more distinguished than I ever was). After having served in the army during World War II, he wasn't keen on getting back to law and was hired as President of Eagle-Lion Films. His main achievement in the business began when he and his partner Robert S. Benjamin assumed management control of United Artists in 1951. That company had originally been founded by Mary Pickford, Charlie Chaplin, D.W. Griffith and Douglas Fairbanks in 1919, but this story is told in full in Tino Balio's brilliant book *United Artists: The Company That Changed the Film Industry* published in 1987 (from which much of my knowledge is derived).

In 1955 Krim and his partners bought out Charlie Chaplin and in 1956, Mary Pickford. In 1957 the company went public and by the time Krim finally left UA in 1977, it had set the all time film industry records for theatrical film rentals ($318m) and was market leader.

Krim invented a structure that endeavoured to combine financial discipline with maximum creative autonomy. This involved backing independent producers and not getting into production centrally and only doing centrally what was best done by a corporation – finance, marketing and distribution. The independent producer, in return for receiving finance, was given a large degree of autonomy, once they had agreed the story of the movie, the cast, the director and the budget with Krim. It was central to the financial structure of United Artists, that they made their money, not just on the production of movies, but on the world-wide distribution margin that they were able to generate. For example, UA financed some hundred–plus pictures up to 1957. Their participation in the profits of the movie themselves amounted to only $24,145. However their profits altogether, before tax, rose from $350,000 to over $6m.

Krim's method of evaluating a profit and deciding whether or not to back it, was a version of what we at PolyGram called 'The Control Sheet'. He was very aware that juggling the price of a movie was one of the most important decisions; an expensive movie may be a better bet than a cheaper one. Potential profit and potential loss were critical issues.

It's interesting to note how the system worked when one looks at the Bond movies. *Doctor No* (1963) had a budget of £1.2m and grossed $6m – a medium success taking into account marketing costs as well. *From Russia With Love* (1963) cost $2m and did better than *Doctor No*. *Goldfinger* (1964) cost $3m and eventually budgets rose to the giddy heights of $16m.

Another important consideration was short lines of communication so that decisions, whether positive or negative, were communicated to the independent producers expeditiously.

As a result, Krim and his management team slowly but surely managed to attract a remarkable roster of talent and independent producers. In the period 1957 to 1962, the company released roughly 40 films a year on average and had approximately 50 independent producers under contract. The principal suppliers were the (now largely forgotten) Mirisch Corporation, which delivered 67 pictures in 18 years, and Broccoli-Saltzman (who are still remembered as the producers of James Bond). The third great supplier was Stanley Kramer who produced *High Noon, On The Beach, Inherit The Wind, Judgement At Nuremberg* and *It's A Mad, Mad, Mad, Mad World* among many others. Among the Mirisch titles were *Some Like It Hot, The Apartment, The Magnificent Seven, West Side Story, The Great Escape, Irma La Douce, The Pink Panther, A Shot In The Dark, Cast A Giant Shadow, The Thomas Crown Affair, Fiddler On The Roof, Scorpio* and many others.

ARTHUR KRIM

Burt Lancaster had a very successful UA based company called Hecht–Hill–Lancaster which made such movies as *Sweet Smell Of Success, Separate Tables, The Unforgiven* and *Birdman Of Alcatraz*. UA won best picture Oscars five times during the 1960's and in 1959 won twelve Oscars out of 19 categories.

Although I didn't start in the business until 20 years after the end of UA under Krim, there is hardly an aspect of the way he ran UA that did not contain a lesson for me in building up PolyGram.

It was not until reading Balio's book, that I realised that, even in the days when the film market outside North America was not as developed or as attractive as it is today, Krim and his partners were deeply involved in the world outside Hollywood. In the 1960's, UA backed the French Company Les Films Ariane (run by Alexandre Mnouchkine, who in turn worked with directors such as Claude Lelouch) to whose product UA had non-US rights. Louis Malle brought them *Viva Maria* starring Brigitte Bardot and Jeane Moreau. They also backed Francois Truffaut.

In Italy, they backed Dino DeLaurentiis and Alberto Grimaldi – the latter bought them the early Clint Eastwood movies *Fistful of Dollars, A Few Dollars More* and *The Good, The Bad, And The Ugly*. Most famously, Grimaldi produced *Last Tango In Paris* with Mariah Schneider and Marlon Brando.

The seeds of the end of United Artists were sown in 1967, when they merged with a Trans-America Corporation. Conglomerates were in style and Krim and his team were seduced by the idea of becoming part of one and obtaining the benefits of the rise in their share price. In a sense, Trans-America was Krim's version of what Philips was to do to me ten years later. The pressure on Krim's team became intolerable and they all handed in their notice and left. Although they thereafter set up Orion Pictures, the world had changed. The capital they had was insufficient and their world-wide reach could not compete with the other major studios and, eventually, Orion folded. Krim had also turned his attention to Democratic politics.

But his searing talent and vision and the remarkable company he formed remain, in my view, one of the great examples of how to do things in Hollywood. An example that should not be forgotten, particularly in the film business, where history and tradition are neither much taught, nor respected.

11
Lew Grade

In 1995 we bought the ITC Entertainment Groups Film and TV catalogue, which comprised, for the most part, television programming and some films made by ATV, one of the pre-eminent UK Independent Broadcasters (while they were run by Lew Grade). I first smelled Lew Grade (rather than saw him) when I was a teenager. I had a holiday job as a tea boy at ATV Headquarters near Marble Arch. I had to get in really early, about 7 am. But way ahead of me in the office was Lew Grade. The reason I smelt him and never saw him was that he had his own tea lady, but was already into his first Monte Cristo No. 2 at that hour.

It's hard to remember now how dominant Lew Grade was in the British Entertainment Industry and what an apparent stranglehold he had on it, together with his brothers, the agent, Leslie Grade, and the impresario, Bernie Delfont. Their history was pure schmaltz. The children of Russian-Jewish immigrants (with a formidable mother, of whom it was said, in later years, was the only woman the Queen of England was afraid of) they were soon into show business. Lew Grade had in fact been world champion Charleston dancer in the 1920's and I believe he was still the reigning champion when he died. He had held the title at the time the championships were abolished. After a long period in agency, Lew, almost by accident, found himself owning a large part of and running ATV, one of the first and pioneering independent TV broadcasters in the United Kingdom. His story and that of the family was told in his own autobiography, *Still Dancing*, and in the autobiography of his nephew Michael Grade.

Courtesy UBA

LEW GRADE

In my mind, Lew stood out as one of the few great entertainment entre-preneurs ever to have worked in the United Kingdom. He was the force behind many TV series that have become legendary on a world-wide basis – such as *The Prisoner* and *Thunderbirds*. He invented the British version of variety entertainment – *Sunday Night at the London Palladium*. He assembled one of the greatest music publishing catalogues, post-Second World War to date – ATV Music. He formed a very successful record company called Pye Records. He produced one of the biggest inter-national high profile television dramas ever made: *Jesus Of Nazareth*. He produced Oscar winning films such as *On Golden Pond* and *Sophie's Choice*. My favourite of all was *The Muppets*.

Unlike most of his colleagues in commercial television in the United Kingdom, he had an international outlook, an unparalleled talent as a salesman and marketeer and, most of all, combined attributes now out of fashion, but nonetheless to be treasured above all in business: truthfulness (with a good dose of cunning thrown in), passion, unswerving devotion to the principle of keeping one's word, internationalism, lack of pretension, and a sense of fun. He also had 'Chutzpah' to a remarkable degree.

And so it was, that when we acquired the ITC catalogue, I asked him if he would consider coming back as President for life as a consultant for us. He readily agreed. Within a few days of agreeing what I thought was a quite generous deal for him, I had a call from Alain Lévy, who, in turn, had a call from Jerrold Perenchio, Lew's great friend and perhaps the biggest mover and shaker in Hollywood. Lew had said to Jerry that he thought the deal was not good enough. Jerry had called Alain, my boss, and ensured I had to pay Lew five times what I had originally suggested.

The punch-line to this story is that, far from being a name on the notepaper, Lew repaid me many times over. Stewart Till and I had long planned a trip to Germany to obtain an output deal for our films in that country. The pre-eminent power in the land was Leo Kirch who, through his various TV interests, has been the dominant acquirer of German rights to Hollywood feature films. Somehow or other, Lew heard of our proposed trip and insisted on coming. He assured us he had known Leo for many years and he would help. We had to spend the night in Munich. Stewart and I (some 40 years younger than Lew) had spent the evening chasing his vast disappearing back down airport corridors and through immigration halls. He hailed a taxi in Yiddish, which he considered must be understood by any modern German taxi driver, even if Lew's Yiddish was learned in the Russian pale some eighty years earlier. At dinner, he would put his napkin over vegetables because he couldn't bear the sight of them. Meat, ice-cream and everything that a modern diet is supposed to avoid was the stuff he liked best.

The next day we met Leo Kirch and his colleagues. The minute we entered the room, Leo and Lew fell about each other's necks with much kissing. Lew spoke some kind of Yiddish to Leo, who talked back in German. They understood each other.

Stewart and I made our long presentation and felt it had gone rather well. Perhaps we would get a deal together in the course of the next two or three months. This was not good enough for Lew. He got up, got hold of Leo and said 'Well, do my boys have a deal?'. They then disappeared into a corner of the room, shook hands and Lew came back to tell us that we had a deal. We still could not believe it. But it was true. It was a very large deal, one of the biggest I have ever done of that nature and Lew was solely responsible for bringing it home. It was an astonishing achievement for a man in his mid-eighties. A second example of the pay-off we received, was when Lew heard we'd sold some of our films to Channel 4. 'What price did we get?' he asked. We told him. 'Nonsense!'. He was off to Channel 4 and what he did there I do not know. I held my breath as we thought the deal was exceptionally good. But, sure enough, he was back within a couple of days having increased it by about a quarter.

By the time Lew's 90th birthday came along, I was based in Los Angeles. After a small conference with Jerry Perenchio, we decided to give Lew a big 90th birthday party in Los Angeles at Jerry's wonderful house in Bel Air. My role was the rather limited one of footing some of the bill. Jerry, as usual, did the most magnificent job of organising. Lew's wife, Kathie, and his nephew Michael flew out to Los Angeles for the occasion. It was held on Friday the 28th of February 1997. Lew drank water while we ploughed our way through Jerry's Corton Charlemagme 1992, Maison Louis Latour, his Chateaux Petrus 1977, his Chateaux D'Yquem 1967 and his Fonseca Port 1948. At the end, Lew made a wonderful speech, without any notes, to a party which included Rupert Murdoch, Michael Eisner, Lew Wasserman, Barry Diller, Norman Lear, Jack Nicholson, Andy Williams, Carole Bayer-Sager, Kirk Kerkorian, Bob Daly, Sidney Poitier and many others. They had all come to pay tribute to a remarkable man.

Shortly thereafter, Lew died, and I miss him greatly to this day. His vast knowledge of the business; his huge enthusiasm for life; his inability to say a bad word about anybody including Robert Holmes à Court who deprived him of his beloved company ATV; his inability to go back on his word; his love of England and everything to do with the entertainment business; his unequalled capacity for creating life-long friends; his generosity in all things – all of these presented a wonderful example.

Too often, his easy to caricature features and cigar made people take him less seriously than they might. Not I.

12
Of colleagues

Every year at PolyGram (when we weren't bust), we held annual conventions in exotic locations. They were necessary evils – in turns intolerably boring and fun. They cost a fortune. Most of the time was spent inside an air conditioned auditorium watching interminable presentations and music videos. However, as anyone who's been in an international company will tell you, while pep talks, lectures, information, budget issues and so forth are the reasons given for these congregations, the real reason is the human intercourse (in the good old fashion sense of that word) that occurs.

Roger Ames, now head of Warner Music, could be counted on to enliven our sessions.

A man who subsequently became a good friend of his and mine, David Munns, was a recent recruit from EMI. He decided to impress our convention in Palm Springs with a didactic and learned discourse on international marketing. That year we experimented by having a television monitor beside each attendee's seat so they could follow more closely the speaker's presentation.

Roger Ames was at that time, I believe, running his own company, London Records, under the aegis of our UK music operation. Roger was notoriously bright, good creatively and as cynical an executive as ever there was, born in Trinidad and trained by EMI. After ten minutes of the presentation, Roger disappeared and a few minutes later images on the TV screens changed from slides of marketing and data to a note saying 'This man is a noodle', 'What crap!' and so forth. Of course, it took some time for the speaker to realise what the enormous hilarity was about and Roger's standing went up considerably. The story illustrates the peculiar ethos of these conferences. They were uncool in the sense that no self respecting creative person would want to attend such a corporate affair. On the other hand, being a participant was a recognition of status. On the third hand, cynicism was the order of the day. And yet one's performance at these conferences was critical to one's continued standing in the group. Roger's method of operation was brilliant, as it played well to all political constituencies.

In later years, another regular attendee was Chris Blackwell, the founder of the Island Group of companies. Born in Jamaica with an upper crust background, Noel Coward living nearby to his family house at Goldeneye, he was obviously a golden boy. He began selling imported records from America in Jamaica to dance bands, moved to England and bought with him acts such as Millie. He was most famous for signing, among others, U2, Bob Marley, Cat Stevens and many other great names of the sixties, seventies and eighties. The sale of his company to PolyGram brought him great riches, but also the frustration of having to fit into a corporate culture. He cultivated a certain air of mystery and 'coolness'. He is the only person I know who regularly flies in flip flops, jeans, tee shirt, jacket and no other luggage at all. I subsequently found out that it takes scores of people to keep you on the road in this style. But it was certainly glamorous. His enthusiasm for people was intense and often short-lived, but his taste in houses and hotels here was immaculate. Whatever criticisms there may have been of him paled into insignificance against the achievements and stature he held in the business.

So often in business, one notices that the giants are frustrated by powerful bureaucrats who, shortly after having caused the most frustration, are no more. It is hard to even remember their names, yet it is difficult to over estimate the frustration they cause to figures of stature. Eventually Chris had enough and left Island behind him to regain his independence.

Courtesy RGA

CHRIS BLACKWELL

Among the other regulars at our conferences were Jan Timmer and (in later years) his successor as President of Phillips, Cor Boonstra. Here is an example of what I mean. Within the music industry, Jan Timmer will always be associated with the successful launch of CD Audio, which saved the industry. As explained in earlier chapters, he not only intro- duced CD Audio, but saved PolyGram and began the turn around of Philips. Maybe it was inevitable that a new force was needed at Philips to take over from him. But nonetheless, few could measure up to Jan.

13
Talent

For several years while in Los Angeles, I held an annual fundraising event at my house in the Hollywood Hills. It came about in this way: the Sundance Institute on whose board I served, needed to raise sufficient money to pay for their marvellous courses. All board members committed to do what they could to raise this money. I knew that to ask the Studios to contribute would be a lost cause. Every week studio heads receive dozens of invitations to charity events and have to take tables costing $10,000 or more because the event is honouring one of their key actors or directors or producers. There was no way they were going to support the Sundance Institute.

However, I felt that the international community owed a lot to the talent that Sundance generated and should contribute. I therefore came up with the idea of hosting a party at my house at the time of the American Film Market, when all international buyers came to Los Angeles to buy films. I would offer them tickets at $1,000 per head to meet stars. The theory was great. In practice however, by the Friday before the Monday on which the party was to be held, I had one hundred assorted international buyers coming to the house for a great dinner to meet stars. The hitch was that I had no stars. I panicked. I rang all my production companies and told them that they would never get the green light on any movie they wanted to make unless they delivered stars on the Monday. And sure enough, on the Monday, we had an 'A' list turn out of stars and raised $80,000 for Sundance.

Every year we went through the same trauma and every year, the quality of the talent turning up improved. In our best year, I think we had Michael Douglas, Jodie Foster, Brad Pitt, Geena Davis, Renee Harlin, David Fincher, Michael Bay and many others among the champagne sipping crowds.

At the last party I gave, I arrived home late, jumped in the shower, only to hear the door bell going with no-one answering it, despite the fact there were dozens of people setting up the party. I grabbed the towel, rushed downstairs and slung open the door to find Brad Pitt waiting on the doorstep, having arrived half an hour early.

The lesson I learnt from organising these parties, was that to try and get stars to turn up by asking them a month or so ahead of time was useless. If there was nothing else to do on a cold Monday evening in Los Angeles they would show up. Once there, they were very professional in buttering up executives who control their fortunes, in the increasingly important international market place. By and large, most actors, whether on stage or screen, put all their talent into creating characters on stage; off stage the best actors are often the least interesting and some of the least interesting actors are the best characters. There are however exceptions. I got to know Robert Redford through our joint venture – the Sundance Channel. Redford has been a star longer than almost anybody in Hollywood, other than Warren Beatty. He has put back more into the industry than almost any of his contemporaries. He founded and ran the Sundance Festival and the Sundance Institute with its teaching courses for writers, performers, directors and producers. He's also one of the most rewarding but frustrating people to work with. He's notoriously late. As my grandfather would have said 'He'll be late for his own funeral'. He is capricious in the sense that, if his gut tells him something is wrong, whatever the business reasons may be, he's hard to budge, even when you know he's wrong. I had a massive task on my hands to convince him to accept an excellent executive for the Sundance Channel who did not give out the right 'vibes'. Whatever Redford's faults, he's forgiven almost everything because of his passion for film and film-makers.

Earlier on I wrote about how much Jodie Foster meant to the success of PolyGram in America. She represents the modern actor who can turn on star power at will. One minute one could walk down a street with her and no-one would recognise her. The next moment, she would turn on the power (without any change of clothes, make-up or the like) and stop people in their tracks. Isabella Rossellini would sit at a table in the public rooms at a hotel in Cannes and no-one would know she was there.

She would then appear for our evening screening of *Wild at Heart* and the assembled masses would fall to their knees. It is hard to imagine that this ability to turn star appeal on and off could have been something familiar to Elizabeth Taylor or Marlene Dietrich.

ROBERT REDFORD

Among the stars, there is another distinguishing characteristic between those who have substance and those who do not. It is an attribute no different to that found in normal life, between those who are smart and those who are not. That is the ability to be a great listener. Redford had the ability to suck information out of you and listen in such an intense way as to be almost exhausting. Similarly, Michael Douglas and Robin Williams. In the few contacts I had with them, they had that interest in others that one rarely comes across. It is the mark of what makes people successful in business.

Sometimes one was surprised that one could have friends or, at least feel one had friends, among the stars.

Joel and Ethan Coen and their families were people we felt immediately at home with. There are few more admired directors than the Coens, few more admired actresses than Joel's wife, Frances McDormand (the Oscar-winning heroine of *Fargo*). But they retain much of their feet-on-the-ground, mid-western American attitude to life and people. However, there is the added thrill, not common with one's more normal friends, of knowing that underneath the everyday family type relationship, run deep creative well-springs which one will never know about or experience except through their art. This tension between 'everydayness' and creative genius is a common (or at least common to me) aspect of the most exceptional among creative people. Richard Curtis, who must be the most brilliant of current British comedy writers, is at one and the same time Mr Ordinary and the most difficult character to comprehend. It's the stuff of stardom.

JOEL AND ETHAN COEN

14
Politicians

In the United States, where there is a strong film industry, one only comes across politicians when they want money to run for office, or when they want to make headlines by opposing the lyrics on albums or alleged conspiracies to corrupt youth.

In Europe, where there is a weak film industry, there are more politicians and industry bodies than you can shake a stick at. I have, by and large, tried to avoid them, but not always successfully. The problem that both British and European politicians fail to grasp is simply stated: we will never have a European based studio that competes with Hollywood, unless it is properly capitalised with world-wide marketing and distribution power. This could be arranged by the British Government or Brussels, but there is too little political gain and too much political risk involved, to ensure that any effective action is taken.

Let's take a simple 'back of an envelope' working example to illustrate what I mean: assume that you've made a film costing $5m, which has a big international success (obviously relative to the size of the movie). Assume for example, that the international box office receipts worldwide amount to $70m. Roughly speaking, the amount the distributor can expect to get back from the theatrical box office is approximately a third. In this case assume $23m. Industry figures indicate that box office receipts comprise approximately a quarter of total receipts, so in this case, the world-wide receipts could be estimated at approximately $90m. From that, we have to take off world-wide prints and advertising costs of say $25m, video duplication and other costs of $10m, commissions, fees, publicity costs and other unspecific costs of another $10m. This would leave you with approximately $45m. Let's make another assumption – that I am way, way over optimistic on my income side and too pessimistic on my cost side. Let's bring down that figure to $30m. Now imagine this is the only hit film you have in a package of ten movies you make, all budgeted in the $5 – $10m range. It would mean that however badly the other movies in the package did, the likelihood is that this package of movies would overall be very successful and be a happy experience for the investor. However, the same movie, made in the way that we make movies in Europe, now means that all the profits go to the international distributors who co-fund the movie and they would be lucky if the financiers of the movie would see back $2-3m net without a structure, such as studios have, to capture the international profit margins. You can therefore see that if you only make two or three million dollars on a hit movie, the chances of a whole package of movies of similar budgets coming out profitably are negligible.

The problem is exacerbated the higher the budget of the movie one makes.

It is not very difficult to understand; nor should it be beyond the powers of the very rich countries that make up the European Union (or even just one of them) to structure something to make sure that we can have a consistently profitable UK or European film operation.

It is a story I've tried to pedal for five years within Europe, to little response. I sat on a high powered committee chaired by the European Commissioner in charge of DG10 with responsibility for film. My recommendations were taken up in his report, but nothing much has come of it. I have had numerous conversations on the subject with Chris Smith, the then UK Minister of Culture. Charming, smart, affable, well respected, it always seemed to me that, because he was first and foremost a politician, he would rather shuffle the problem on to someone else's plate rather than take the high profile, high risk road of putting right what really needs to be put right in the British Film Industry. While of course I applaud the tax breaks given in the UK to the film industry and the money and better co-ordination that has been brought about by the establishment of the Film Council in the UK, I very much fear that the whole thing is doomed to failure (albeit the Government are seeing to it that if such failure occurs it cannot be laid at their door). For the reasons I have given, it's rather dispiriting, but this has not prevented me from continuing to bang this particular drum and try to set up myself, together with commercial interests, what Governments refuse to do.

I'll conclude with a little story of how mad the workings of politics and film can be. When I returned from the USA, the Film Council in the UK was about to be set up. I knew that my friend, the film director Alan Parker, was very keen to assume the Chairmanship of that Body and I welcomed this, as he is a very able person and a real artist. As I was settling into my new life back in England, I had a call from a top Civil Servant at the Culture Ministry. Would I put my name forward to be Chairman of the Film Council? I said I thought one had to volunteer and I had not volunteered. He said, 'Ah, but we just need you to put your name forward because we wanted a real choice'. I said I would only put my name forward at their request, if it was not to compete with Alan Parker. They said they understood that, but it would be useful even if they appointed Alan Parker to say they had considered other people such as myself. Busy with other matters, I didn't think about it too much and said, 'Okay put my name forward on that basis'. The next thing was a receipt in the post of a huge form to be filled in by me as a condition of my name going forward. I rang up the Civil Servant again, 'What on earth is all this about. I don't want to apply, I didn't apply, you asked me to give my name, to let my name go forward and that's enough'. 'Oh well' he said, 'Just fill in the odd thing and send it back to help us out'. I did this. Next I was summonsed to an interview for the job of Chairman for the Film Council. By this time I was beyond bemused. In any event I turned up and said I hadn't applied, thought that Alan Parker would make an excellent Chairman and so on and so forth and left. Then I was rung up by a junior Minister while I was on holiday in Sardinia. 'I'm so sorry', the Minister said, 'I'm afraid you haven't been successful in your application to be Chairman of the Film Council!'. I said that I never applied for this job … 'Well', she said, 'how about being on the Council itself?'. Enough was enough and I resolved to keep out of such things in the future, as they seem to have nothing to do with anything except politics and they are certainly nothing to do with the trials and tribulations of the British Film Industry.

PART THREE

Some other bit-parts observed

15
The control sheet

I developed the control sheet (see page 130) together with Malcolm Ritchie at PolyGram.

The purpose of this sheet was to have all the key considerations that went into approving a movie on one piece of paper. Although it looks complicated, it isn't. The reason it's worth looking at is, not only to show how we viewed the profitability of movies, but also, as I will explain shortly, it shows how any fully integrated studio looks at movie profitability.

The sheet is divided into three main sections. In the top section there is a summary of who the director is, the cast, the producer, the start date and other details, but most particularly, a summary of the amount payable to those cast members and other key talent who participate in the gross or net profits of a film. BO means Box Office. CBE means Cash Break Even. IAB means Initial Actual Breakeven. The next box in the top section summarises the above the line costs, (meaning actors, directors, writers, producers, etc.) and below the line costs (the actual cost of physical production). There is a provision for a contingency and, in this case, there is also a provision for a completion bond. One then adds on the producers fee and finance cost to reach the total negative cost. In the right-hand box one can see whether the movie is being made under any of the relevant Guild agreements (in this case American Guilds) because there then follow certain consequences for residual and health and welfare benefit payments.

In the next section down, there is an overall summary showing the sensitivity analysis of the movie at various US and non-US box office results. In the case in question, one can see that breakeven on this movie, which costs around $20m, is reached at a US box office of about $30m with an equal foreign box office.

In the third section, there is a break-down of the constituent income streams that make up the summary contained in section 2. It will be seen that there is a distinction made between domestic gross box office (the United States and Canada) and US gross box office (restricted to the USA alone). The next line down shows the Rental Rate. The Rental Rate is the percentage of the income paid by the cinema-goers to the exhibitor which reaches the studio. This varies considerably from studio to studio, but in general, a block-buster type movie that does much of its business in its initial weeks of exhibition, attracts a higher percentage of exhibitor revenue than an art movie, which finds its audience over a longer period of time.

The next section deals with the number of home video units sold at rental and sell through. More recently, particularly in the USA, revenue sharing between retail outlets and the distributor has become prevalent; but this is still a useful method of looking at the revenue to be expected from home video and various levels of box office.

Pay Television income will depend on the particular deal that the studio has with the American Pay TV services such as Home Box Office and Show Time. Whether one gets a network sale is very much a hit and miss affair. On big important movies, this income can be very substantial, while some movies are completely un-sellable at any price to network television.

Basic cable and syndication income comes next. This is a growing segment of the income stream, but is only achieved in later years.

International advances represent income achieved from those territories where PolyGram did not have its own direct distribution. In more recent times, most studios have tried to protect their down side risk and conserve capital, by selling off major territories internationally (sometimes all territories outside the United States) and, if they are not involved in a joint venture where all revenues come into a pot which is split after distribution fees, then any such income would appear in this line.

International direct income refers to the amount received at studio headquarters from national organisations, after their distribution fees (such as are allowed by the studio) are deducted.

The last items in this section relate to the costs and are self-explanatory for the most part. International marketing costs have been rising alarmingly – perhaps not quite as badly as those in the United States, but they still represent between a third and a half of US marketing costs. 'Residuals' refers to the amount payable to Unions and 'Participation' refers to the amount payable to talent who have a significant stake in revenues or profits.

Once I had established this form of control and assessment of projects at PolyGram, I tried to ensure that every part of the organisation became involved in the development of this control sheet and was giving input. Thus, as soon as a movie looked as though it might be a candidate for green lighting, the producer would start working up the proposal – getting feedback from the international territories where we distributed movies ourselves, from the sales division in respect of those territories that we sold to third parties, from the US marketing people with regard to how much P&A would be required and whether the mid-case box office scenario was realistic and so on. The purpose was to have everyone invested in the process of deciding whether or not to make a movie.

That did not mean to say that the green lighting of a movie depended mechanically on the control sheet; it did, however, become an indispensable tool in making an informed decision and getting most parts of the organisation to understand how such decisions were made.

The structure of this control sheet evolved over time from the format here and considerable effort was continually given to upgrading it.

As I went about my business, I further distilled the results of each green lit film onto a small card which I kept in my briefcase, so that anywhere, at anytime, I could remind myself of our intentions when we approved the film and compare it to the actuality.

POLYGRAM FILMED ENTERTAINMENT   *CONTROL SHEET MASTER*
Production Control Sheet - Summary

FILM DETAILS		PRODUCTION BUDGET ($000)		DRAFT NOTES	
Director	A. Smithee	Above-the-Line	$3,600		
Cast	A. Starr	Below-the-Line	7,200		
Producer	A. Producer	Sub-Total	10,800		
Start Date	01-Jan-98				
Estimated Release Date	01-Mar-99	Contingency 0.0%	0		
Distributor	Studio	Completion 1.3%	140		
Pay TV Deal?	High	Sub-Total	10,940	**RESIDUALS**	
Network TV Sale?	Yes			Guilds: SAG	Y
Participations:		Label Fee 15.0%	1,500	WGA	Y
A. Starr: $5M against 5% of 1st Dollar Gross; BO kick		PFE Fee 2.5%	250	DGA	Y
A. Smithee: 5% of CBE w/10% fee; esc. to 7.5% of CB		Finance Costs	453	AFM	Y
esc. to 10% @ IAB.		**Total Negative Cost**	**$13,143**	IATSE	Y

SUMMARY ($000)	LOW			MEDIUM			HIG
U.S. Gross Box Office	$20,000	$25,000	$30,000	$35,000	$40,000	$45,000	$50,0(
Non U.S. Box Office	85,524	99,446	113,367	127,289	137,546	147,803	158,0(
% of U.S. Box Office	427.6%	397.8%	377.9%	363.7%	343.9%	328.5%	316.
Income before Fee Contribution	$23,324	$27,300	$30,613	$23,324	$38,805	$43,068	$46,8(
Fee Contribution	15,838	17,462	19,045	20,591	21,970	23,464	24,9(
Income after Fee Contribution	$39,162	$44,763	$49,658	$43,914	$60,775	$66,531	$71,8(
Return before Fee Contribution	68.4%	74.2%	76.6%	55.8%	89.3%	95.5%	100.4
Return after Fee Contribution	114.8%	121.7%	124.3%	105.0%	139.9%	147.6%	153.8

NET INCOME ANALYSIS ($000)	LOW			MEDIUM			HIGH
Domestic Gross Box Office	$22,000	$27,000	$33,000	$38,000	$43,000	$49,000	$54,0(
U.S. Gross Box Office	$20,000	$25,000	$30,000	$35,000	$40,000	$45,000	$50,0(
Rental Rate	40.0%	41.0%	42.5%	42.5%	42.5%	44.0%	45.
U.S. Home Video Units - Rental	180	200	215	230	245	260	2;
U.S. Home Video Units - Sell-Thru	20	25	30	40	60	80	1;
Rental Income	$8,000	$10,250	$12,750	$14,875	$17,000	$19,800	$22,5(
Net Home Video Receipts · $41.00	7,380	8,200	8,815	9,430	10,045	10,660	11,2;
Net Home Video Receipts · $4.00	80	100	120	160	240	320	4(
Pay TV Gross Receipts	4,450	5,643	6,568	7,354	7,840	8,456	9,0(
PPV Gross Receipts	156	204	252	288	324	352	3;
Network Gross Receipts	1,000	1,250	1,500	2,000	2,500	2,750	3,0(
Basic Cable Gross Receipts	450	500	550	600	650	825	1,0(
Syndication Gross Receipts	185	195	205	213	225	238	2(
Non-Theatrical Receipts	0	0	0	0	0	0	
Merchandising Receipts	0	0	0	0	0	0	
International Advances	21,009	21,009	21,009	21,009	21,009	21,009	21,0(
International Direct Income	28,270	31,484	34,698	37,911	40,443	42,975	45,5(
Total Receipts	70,980	78,834	86,466	93,840	100,276	107,385	114,4
Negative Costs	13,143	13,143	13,143	13,143	13,143	13,143	13,14
U.S. P&A Costs	13,780	15,900	18,550	19,875	21,200	22,525	23,8!
International P&A Costs	7,187	7,726	8,264	8,803	9,111	9,419	9,7;
Theatrical Distribution Fee 15.0%	1,200	1,538	1,913	2,231	2,550	2,970	3,3;
Home Video Distribution F 20.0%	1,431	1,592	1,714	1,841	1,978	2,114	2,2;
TV Fees (15% except 25% on synd & ba	1,000	1,238	1,437	1,650	1,818	1,999	2,1;
PFI Fee (5% on Direct/15% on Subs)	4,205	4,339	4,473	4,607	4,718	4,829	4,9<
PFI Sales Costs	600	600	600	600	600	600	6(
Residuals	5,109	5,457	5,759	6,075	6,353	6,615	6,8(
Participations	0	0	0	0	0	103	6(
Total Disbursements	47,656	51,533	55,853	58,825	61,471	64,317	67,5(
Film Income before Fee Contribution	**$23,324**	**$27,300**	**$30,613**	**$23,324**	**$38,805**	**$43,068**	**$46,8(**

The Control Sheet

16
Opening a movie in America

There are not many businesses in which the executive team discover whether or not their new product is a hit or a miss in the course of an afternoon.

Most studios make fifteen to twenty movies a year that may be considered main-stream big budget movies. Nowadays, the average Hollywood studio movie costs approximately $40m and the marketing costs just to get the movie open would usually exceed $20m. Accounting rules are such, that if on the first weekend it appears that the movie is going to be a flop, a large part of that $60m investment has to be written off immediately. Even for the large corporations who own US studios, such a 'hit' to the bottom line is tough to endure.

The pressure to avoid having to take such a blow has led to various developments in the business: most studios now cover their down side risk by joint venturing investments in movies. They either sell off international rights for a disproportionately high part of the budget or they joint venture on a pool basis with another studio. For example, Fox may take domestic distribution rights and Paramount international distribution rights. Each may take a fee off the top and then divide costs and revenues equally thereafter. In this way the down side is protected and if the movie is a success a certain amount of up side can be retained.

US studios become ever more dependent on the growth in the international markets hoping that the poor margins in the US market may be recovered by better margins internationally.

Many financing structures have been generated to smooth earnings or take investments off the balance sheet of the studio.

But, most importantly, the marketing and distribution of movies has become a gut wrenching, drawn out, highly sophisticated, full of bullshit process lasting months and months.

Bringing the movie to market

Once a rough cut of a film with a temporary soundtrack is ready, movies are tested. This involves recruiting an audience of the target demographic, usually somewhere on the out-skirts of Los Angeles, New York or a major city such as Dallas.

A nervous executive team and an even more nervous producer and director show up for the screening. The company called National Research Group has a monopoly of organising these screenings. An eager representative of NRG will introduce the film and hand out score cards when the film has finished. A discussion group is then held with twenty or so members of the audience. These scores, while disparaged by everyone in the business, are, in truth, the lodestar by which most executive decisions are taken.

There follows (in most cases) much activity intended to improve the scores at subsequent screenings.

Meantime, a campaign is put together which comprises many disparate elements, such as: how are you going to get the movie noticed? Basically, this requires a large amount of expenditure on electronic media such as TV and radio, and sometimes, outdoor advertising, newspaper ads and the like.

Assuming one is able to devise a plan whereby most of the country knows your movie is opening, you still have to convince them that the movie is worth going to. This requires creative input: the poster, the trailer, the TV ad, the radio spot. All of these must be such that the movie looks as though it is something that you would like to go and see. Most important of all these is the TV spot and the creative department gets together with outside vendors. Once they have come up with a whole series of spots, these again are tested. The important issue here is the increase in interest between the score the movie gets when just mentioning title stars and subject matter to the test audience and their reaction once they have seen the teaser. The poster always causes the most argument, because everyone is familiar with film posters which are often the only survivors of the advertising campaign. In truth, it's relatively unimportant in the marketing process, but very important for hanging on your wall later.

Once you've got the answer as to how you should spend your money to gain the biggest audience and are confident that your creative materials are such that, once they know about your movie, an audience is going to show up, one needs to track how you are doing as you march on towards the opening date. Again, a mechanism is there to help you – tracking reports. These measure awareness of films and their 'want-to-see' factor on certain dates and their relative strength, compared to other films opening on a similar date. You have to keep your eye on this, to see whether you need to spend more on advertising because other companies are spending excessively, to draw attention to their own movies. It is also important to be aware of how movies that open immediately before you are doing and the strength of movies opening in the weeks immediately after your own movie opens.

The combination of all the foregoing means that even hardened studio executives work themselves up into a considerable lather in the weeks and days before the Friday on which their movie opens.

If ,as is the case with most studio heads, they are based in Los Angeles, they are able to check on a Friday morning what the figures were for the early shows in New York. By the time they go home that evening, they have a pretty good idea as to whether the movie will open strongly or not. This is followed by a late night call on the Friday from the head of distribution and an early call first thing in the morning. The rest of the weekend, in my case, meant calls from my boss in London, my colleague Stuart Till and various international territories wanting to see how the movie had done. This stress was repeated fifteen to twenty times a year, depending on how many movies one released.

Once a movie is open, you then take exit polls to see how it played and worry weekend after weekend as to how it will hold up and whether you can take the opening number and multiply it by two, three or four to postulate your end box office.

One might have little concern for the over-stressed studio executives, given their vast salary and perks of office; however, this stressful end game concentrates the mind of those who have to decide which movies to make and causes them to be ultra cautious in their choice. It explains much about the homogenised market driven movies that dominate Hollywood's output.

17
African-American films

One of our early successes of our own distribution in America was a small movie called *Posse*. This could most easily be described as an African-American western directed by and starring Mario Van Peebles. Mario's father, Melvyn, who also appeared in *Posse,* was a renowned director of one of the first significant African-American movies, *Sweet Sweetback's Baadasssss Song* (1971).

Encouraged by this success, I thought about setting up an African-American film label to encourage African-American film-making. I talked at length to African-American producers – Doug McHenry and George Jackson. George Jackson, now sadly dead, had been recommended to me by the then chairman of Motown Records, Clarence Avant. Between us, we came to the conclusion that, if we could make African-American films relatively inexpensively, they had a good audience and a good tie-in with the very successful African-American record business.

Our first movie together was one directed by Doug McHenry and produced by George Jackson called *Jason's Lyric*. Although it did not lose us money, it was not a success. We then struggled to find the next project to work on. After a while, it became apparent that the main problem we faced was that marketing an African-American movie was as expensive as marketing any of our films and yet our international distribution organisation could find almost no value for such a movie, thus making the risk almost impossible to accept. With very few exceptions, this has continued to be the situation. In my opinion, the only way it can be resolved is by a concerted effort from African-American film-makers to develop the international market place for their movies, in the same way that Berry Gordy developed the international demand for Motown artistes in the second half of the twentieth century.

18
Television and catalogues

Once we had a significant supply of high profile movies, we felt the need of building a significant catalogue. The reason is simple: catalogues rarely lose their value. They are valued by a multiple of the cash flow they generate. The reliability of this cash flow is ensured, if one has new products in the form of new feature films to add to the catalogue and the new feature films can enhance the cash flow from the catalogue. When you have a huge hit movie, it enables you to sell more catalogue at higher prices and that incremental cash flow gives you additional leverage from the success of your movies. It is a virtuous circle of value building and extracting maximum benefit from hit movies. It was thus we came successfully to bid on the ITC catalogue, being the catalogue built up by Lew Grade and his ATV commercial TV franchise in the UK and the CDR library, which represented a package of many catalogues of independent films financed by Credit Lyonnais. We made unsuccessful bids to buy the Goldwyn film catalogue and the Chinese language Golden Harvest catalogue.

The bulk of the income from catalogues comes from the TV rights, which are sold and resold around the world. This led to a further thought of how we could (and indeed whether we should) venture into television. When we acquired ITC, Jules Haimovitz, who had been brought in to prepare that company for sale, agreed to come and work with me. Before leaving to do further entrepreneurial TV related activities and eventually join MGM, Jules brought all his experience as a former senior executive at Viacom to bear, in helping me formulate a plan to start TV operations for PolyGram.

After much consideration and talking to many people, including the great TV genius Norman Lear, I hired an ICM agent, Bob Sanitsky to put together a plan to develop programming for network, cable and syndicated TV. To teach him the numbers, I put one of our most seasoned financial people, Deana Elwell, at his side and the two began an operation which (had it had time to mature) I felt confident would have developed an excellent TV operation. The core issue in TV is to get enough episodes made so that you can sell the package effectively into syndication in America and international syndication around the world. In most cases, the US TV broadcaster does not pay the full cost of the programme. The producer therefore has to carry the deficit until sufficient programmes are assembled to make a package that's sellable to such customers in the US and internationally and thereby, release the profits that one hopes the programming will generate. This leads to very significant cash requirements. Sanitsky's plan was simple; to try and cover a disproportionately high part of the programme costs from international sales and other sources, so as to make the risk and the cash flows more bearable. His first three series being *Motown Live*, a music show, *The Crow – Stairway to Heaven*, a drama based on the well known movie and *Total Recall – The Series*, again a drama based on a famous movie, were all successful in meeting this game plan.

In addition to Bob Sanitsky's operation, we developed a division of visual programming to acquire and produce original material for video and TV. Run by Hugh Rees-Parnell in London, we had great success with an animated children's series *Masie* based on the children's books, *Cats*, being a film of the famous stage show by Andrew Lloyd-Webber and Michael Flatley's *Feet of Flames*.

Internationally, we established a TV sales operation run by David Ellender and an international merchandising and licensing operation run by Caroline Mickler, in addition to our international film sales operation run by Aline Perry.

The combination of our new films, our growing catalogue, our new own developed TV programming, our international acquisitions and our merchandise and licensing made for a large, growing and predictable value chain that was an essential part of building the studio.

19
Management

PolyGram Films grew from being, in essence, myself and Malcolm Ritchie and a few support staff in Los Angeles, to an organisation employing approximately 1,000 people throughout the world. I saw one of my main tasks in management as laying out the clear vision of the task in hand and of selling it upwards to my board and shareholders, and downwards throughout the organisation.

I held myself accountable to the board and to the organisation to meet goals. If we succeeded, I felt I could take the credit. If we failed, I felt I knew I should take the blame. Similarly, it seemed to me, the fault of the studio system was that success was claimed by everybody and fault was avoided by everybody. It was only if people knew who was responsible and held them accountable, that progress could be made and we could attract the best executives.

Next to myself, Stewart Till was held responsible for all our operations outside North America. Our production entities were given the resources and chose the movies on which to work. It was clear who should claim the credit and who should get the blame. Our national organisations were given as much autonomy as was possible. The head of the organisation could not blame a divisional head for problems in their area. That person running that country was responsible for that country's results.

The selling of the game plan required endless presentations to our management board, our regional organisations, our national organisations and our producers. Constant repetition of the mantra, that we were building a European studio from scratch, was essential.

Although it is always difficult to judge one's success with one's own organisation, I felt considerable pride growing in our accomplishments. The fact that key employees are now highly placed in all areas of the film business world-wide, was some indication of the fact that we developed good people who were widely respected.

Even with our own shareholders, so difficult to convince about the opportunities in the movie business, I felt we made some progress. I learned slowly and painfully the importance of the press in transmitting a more positive image and to establish good relationships with the financial and trade press. I started an annual lunch at the Cannes Film Festival for the UK press and it gradually became a much anticipated and fun event.

The PolyGram of latter years, whether in music or film, was widely perceived to be an organisation with excellent management, that worked in a relatively harmonious and happy environment. There was a conception that Philips sold PolyGram because either it hated Alain Lévy, or hated the music business, or hated the film business, or was jealous of the remuneration given to film and music executives, or any combination of these. However, while there may be some truth to any one of those irritants, the real reason was that Philips management (unlike, say, Jack Welch at GE) were unwilling to learn the business, which had meant so much to Philips' shareholders, and were unsure of themselves to the extent that they did not want to trust the management of PolyGram.

I believe much value was lost to PolyGram and Philips shareholders as a result of this management attitude on the part of Philips.

20
The Sundance Channel

Some 20 years or so ago, Robert Redford took over an ailing film festival in Salt Lake City, moved it to an old Utah mountain mining town called Park City and renamed it The Sundance Film Festival. This is somewhat misleading because Sundance is a small ski resort some 40 minutes from Park City, but in a valley that Redford has been lovingly preserving from modern development for many years.

From small beginnings, the festival has grown to be the leading independent film festival in the world. The profits it makes are fed into the Sundance Institute, which trains young people throughout the year in all aspects of film-making. Somehow, my name was mentioned to Redford as a candidate for the board of the Sundance Institute. Together with my wife, I found myself in Spring 1994 in one of the wonderful log cabins in the woods above Sundance, attending, as an observer, part of one of the teaching courses. A message came from 'The Great One' and I was invited horse riding before breakfast the next day. I don't think Redford realised that Jews and horse riding do not go together, but I was too cowardly to decline. I prayed all night for intervention from on High and sure enough, an incredible storm appeared and riding was cancelled. A breakfast with Redford turned into an invitation to join the board.

In due course, his representatives approached us to join them and Viacom in a joint venture to launch an independent film channel called Sundance, to be carried over cable and satellite. Initially, I turned it down because there was already a good competitor, Independent Film Channel, and I did not believe that one could get people to pay (as they proposed) a separate monthly subscription for an independent film channel. After some time, we were again approached and looked at a channel paid for by the cable and satellite operators, which meant that it was free to the public as part of their monthly subscription. This time it looked do-able. With a loan from us of $31million (giving us a 5 per cent stake), a supply of movies and back office services from Show Time and, with Redford as editor, the Sundance Channel launched in 1996 under the able management of Larry Aidem and his marvellous sales and marketing team.

Although it was a late entry into the discrete channel market, the channel became a huge success and within five years was both profitable and worth in excess of $400million.

Postscript

The story of PolyGram Films is of an endeavour to establish a Hollywood-style studio in London. Whatever else may be said of the effort and of the films we made, one thing is clear: there is no reason why such an endeavour should not have been crowned with success. We set out a blueprint for a European Studio in 1991 and, starting from scratch, the plan was fulfilled within a decade, with all key benchmarks having been met. Whatever rocks I may have anticipated as a danger to our little galleon, 'death by owner' was not one of them.

Encouraged by this experience I am now embarking on a 'new and improved' plan to achieve, in a way that cannot be so undermined, the realisation of my original dream and that of many others before me – Michael Balcon and Alexander Korda among them – a permanently established, world-class film studio operating from London. Our national treasure chest of talent deserves no less.

Appendices

1
The Players

Many of those listed below have since moved to other jobs with other companies. The job titles given here are generally those held during the period covered by this book.

Aidem, Larry
CEO of the Sundance Channel.

Alvero, Rafael
PFE Spain.

Ames, Roger
Chairman of PolyGram's UK operations from 1993. Managing Director of London Records until 1993. Current Chairman of Warner Music.

Aukin, David
Head of Drama and Commissioning Editor of Films at Channel 4. Founding partner of HAL (Miramax) with Colin Leventhal and Trea Hoving.

Backman, Lennart
PFE distribution, Sweden.

Balcon, Michael
(1986-1977) Head of MGM-British then of Ealing Studios. Chairman of British Lion (1964-1968) and of the Experimental Film Fund.

Balian, Haig
PFE Distribution Holland and subsequently Germany.

Bannon, Steve
Bannon & Co. (investment bankers for PFE).

Benjamin, Robert S
Head of United Artists with Arthur Krim (1951-1967).

Bevan, Tim
Co-president of Working Title Films with Eric Fellner.

Biondi Jr., Frank
Chairman and CEO of Universal Studios. Fired by Seagram on 16 November 1998.

Blackwell, Chris
Founder of Island Records.

Blank, Matthew
President Show Time Networks Inc.

Bogart, Neil
Original owner of Casablanca Records. CFO and Joint President, with Peter Guber, of Casablanca Record and FilmWorks.

Boonstra, Cornelis
Chairman of the Board of Management and President of Royal Philips Electronics.

Bradstreet, Graham
Working Title Films.

Brouwer, Chris
PFE Distribution Holland. Haig Balian's partner.

Brecher, Kenneth
Sundance Institute Executive Director (appointed 1st August 1996).

Bridges, Dawn
PFE Corporate Communications.

Bronfman Jr., Edgar
President and CE of Seagram Co.

Burton, Caroline
PFI sales representative and Michael Kuhn's wife.

Cheng, Norman
PolyGram board member. Head of Far East Music.

Clark, Tom
UK Minister for Film and Tourism.

Cook, Jan
Joined PolyGram in 1973 as Domestic Chief Financial Officer. Executive Vice President and Chief Financial Officer of PolyGram N.V. since 1978. Member of the PolyGram Board of Management since 1986. Temporarily took over from Alain Lévy 23 June 1998. Retired from PolyGram on the 8 Dec 1998.

Covo, José
PFE Distribution France.

Cunningham, Eddie
MD PFE Sell-thru (UK).

Curtis, Richard
Scriptwriter of *Four Weddings and a Funeral, Bean, Notting Hill.*

Daugherty, David
PFE Legal & Business Affairs.

De Lille, Dirk
MD PFE Distribution Holland.

Devine, Zanne
Senior VP, PolyGram Filmed Entertainment. Formerly Production VP at Universal and Universal's liaison with Gramercy.

Dick, Nigel
Director of *Private Investigations,* first film made under Michael Kuhn.

Diller, Barry
Chairman and CEO of Twentieth Century Fox (1984-1992). Currently Chairman of USA Networks.

Ditrinco, Linda
Gramercy National Sales VP.

Dobbis, Rick
President, PolyGram International.

Durie, John
Manifesto Film Sales.

Eisner, Michael
Chairman, Walt Disney.

Ells, Stuart
PolyGram Head of Audit. Subsequently CFO/COO in the last few years of PFE.

Elwell, Deana
CFO PFE English language production. Previously TV and film accountant in the USA.

Fellner, Eric
Co-president of Working Title Films in 1992. Founder of Initial Pictures (later Initial Films and Television) in 1985.

Field, Ted
Founder of Interscope Communications.

Fine, David
Chairman of the PolyGram N.V. Supervisory Board (1991-1997). Chairman of International Federation of the Phonographic Industry; CEO of PolyGram's UK operations Feb 1978 until 1983; appointed Executive Vice President and to the Board of Management of PolyGram N.V. in 1987. President and CEO of PolyGram from Jan 1983 until 1991.

Finkelstein, Rick
PFE business deals consultant (ex-Nelson). Now President of Universal Studios.

Fogelson, Andrew
President of PolyGram Filmed Entertainment Distribution. Ex-United Artists.

Foster, Jodie
CEO of Egg Productions with Stewart Kleinman, Head of Production, (ex-ICM) and Julie Bergman (ex-Mirage Productions). Signed to PolyGram: 21 October 1992.

Fryland, Stefan
PFE distribution, Denmark.

Gaydon, John
PolyGram Video/TV International. Involved with EG records and music videos.

Globus, Menahem
President of Cannon Films Inc.

Golan, Yoram
Chairman of Cannon Films Inc.

Golembo, Michael
MD of Channel 5 Video Distribution – PolyGram UK's sell-through video company.

Golin, Steve
Co-president of Propaganda Films. Subsequently founded Anonymous Films.

Grade, (Lord) Lew
Founder of ATV. Former Agent and Chairman of ITC.

Gramatke, Wolf
Head of PolyGram Germany.

Graves, Peter
President of PFE marketing group (ex-Nelson) and subsequently head of marketing at PFED (US).

Gray, Claudia
Head of marketing at Gramercy.

Guber, Peter
Producer at PolyGram Pictures. Chairman of Sony Pictures. Founder of Mandalay Entertainment.

Haas, Eckart
Ran Polygram Pictures. Came from regional TV.

Helfant, Michael
Interscope, Legal and Business now at Fine Line.

Hix, Wolfgang
President and CEO of PolyGram Group (1.1.1981 - 31.12.1982). Member of PG Board of Management since 1987. Consultant to Board of Management since 1983 and General Counsel.

Hockman, David
Started as a lawyer at PolyGram UK at the same time as Michael Kuhn. Founded PolyGram Publishing and now at Edel Music.

Holmes á Court, Robert
An Australian entrepreneur who beguiled Lew Grade into selling him ATV.

James, Dick
Founded Dick James Music (handling The Beatles and Elton John), a company later bought by PolyGram.

Johnssen, Jorn
PFE distribution, Norway.

Juarez, Ele
PFE distribution, Spain.

Kennedy, John
Business Lawyer for PolyGram UK. Ran Universal Music UK.

Kenworthy, Duncan
Producer of *Four Weddings and a Funeral, Bean* and *Notting Hill*. Co-founder of DNA Films.

Kerkorian, Kirk
Sometime MGM owner. Billionaire, entrepreneur and Las Vegas Casinos owner.

Klein, Allen
Sometime Manager of the Beatles and the Rolling Stones.

Korda, Alexander
Founder of London Film Productions in 1932 and one for the fundamental figures in establishing the British film industry.

Krim, Arthur
Head of United Artists.

Kuhn, Michael A
Executive Vice President of PolyGram N.V. and Member of PolyGram Board of Management 1993-1998. Appointed Senior Vice President of PolyGram and President of the Media Division in 1987 (as well as head of New Business Division and Group Legal Counsel); appointed President of PolyGram Filmed Entertainment in 1992. Joined PolyGram in 1974 from media solicitors Denton, Hall & Burgin.

Ladd Jr., Allan
Sometime Chairman of MGM/UA.

Lévy, Alain
President and CEO of PolyGram N.V. (1991-1998) and CEO of PolyGram Holding, Inc. Member of Philips' Board of Management (1990-1998). Appointed CEO of PolyGram's French operations in 1984; appointed Executive VP with responsibility for popular music and music publishing in 1989; appointed member of Group Management Committee of Philips N.V. in 1991.

Mancuso, Frank
Head of Distribution at Paramount until 1991. Chairman of MGM under Kirk Kerkorian until 1999.

Mason, Graham
PFE Head of Acquisitions.

McDonald, Andrew
Producer of *Trainspotting*. Later co-founder of DNA Films with Duncan Kenworthy.

McGurk, Chris
President of Universal Pictures in mid-1998. Head of Strategic Planning at Universal. In charge of the PFE sale to Seagram. Went on to run MGM. Senior VP of Disney in 1988 and at Pepsico before that.

Meyer, Marc
Senior VP Strategic Planning and Business PFE.

Meyer, Ron
President of Universal.

Moore, Jane
CFO Polygram Filmed Entertainment and International Distribution.

Morris, Doug
Head of Universal's Music Group and Chairman, in 1998, of the combined Universal/PolyGram music entity.

Morrison, Angela
CO Working Title Films.

Northcott, Richard
MD of Nelson Entertainment.

Oreja, Marcelino
Member of European Commission. Commissioner for Audiovisual Policy.

Ovitz, Mike
Past Chairman of Creative Artists Agency. Founder of AMG.

Palmer, Wendy
Manifesto Film Sales/CiBy Sales.

Perenchio, Jerrold
Chairman of Univision. Friend of Michael Kuhn and Lévy. Previous owner of Embassy Pictures.

Parretti, Giancarlo
Italian financier. Brief owner of MGM.

Perry, Aline
President of Manifesto Film Sales.

Peters, John
Producer associate of Peter Guber.

Pollock, Dale
President A&M Films. Author of book on George Lucas (*Skywalking: The Life and Films of George Lucas*).

Pollock, Tom
Chairman of the MCA/Universal's Motion Picture Group. Involved with setting up the Gramercy deal. Chairman of the American Film Institute. Started production company with Ivan Reitman in 1998 (Montecito). Formed law firm, Pollock, Bloom & Dekom, in 1971.

Powell, Nik
Scala/Palace Productions. Chairman, European Film Academy.

Punt, Marc
MD PFE Distribution Belgium.

Radclyffe, Sarah
Past Co-president of Working Title Films.

Ravaglione, Filipo
PFE Distribution Italy.

Read, Tim
PVI Australia.

Redford, Robert
President of Sundance Institute and Sundance Channel (Viacom/ Show Time and PolyGram). Actor, director, producer.

Redstone, Sumner
Chairman of Viacom (MTV, VH1, Paramount, Blockbuster, etc.).

Rees-Parnell, Hugh
PFE children's video production.

Reitman, Ivan
Director. Formed production company with Tom Pollock in 1998 – output deal with PolyGram Filmed Entertainment.

Rich, Lee
Sometime Chairman and CEO of MGM/UA. Producer.

Ritchie, Malcolm
COO PolyGram Filmed Entertainment, Partner Kuhn & Co. Ltd.

Rosenfeld, Paul
Gramercy Distribution VP.

Ross, Steve
Founder of Warner Communications.

Rozalla, David
MD of PolyGram Video/TV International.

Sanitsky, Robert
President of PolyGram TV.

Schwartz, Russell
President of Gramercy (1 June 1992). Formerly VP at Miramax and at Island Pictures and Island Alive. Currently at USA Films.

Senardi, Stefano
PFE distribution, Italy.

Sheinberg, Sid
Sometime Chairman of MCA and owner of Universal Studios.

Sighvatsson, Sigurjon ('Joni')
Co-president of Propaganda Films.

Sinclair, Nigel
Lawyer at Denton Hall and later LA film lawyer. Founder of Intermedia with Guy East.

Smith, Chris
UK Secretary of State for Culture.

Smith, Peter
Head of UK PFE theatrical and rental distribution. Now Head of Universal Video outside the US.

Sondheim, Bill
Gramercy video.

Southey, Caroline
PFE VP Literary Rights in 1993. Joined PolyGram in 1988 and was Head of Business Affairs at Working Title from 1991. Alain Lévy's wife.

Stigwood, Robert
Head of Robert Stigwood Organisation (RSO). Involved with music and film and had a joint deal with PolyGram in the 1970s.

Stulberg, Gordon
Formerly lawyer and President of Twentieth Century Fox. Ran PolyGram Pictures under Peters and Guber. Chairman of American Interactive Media.

Tandy, Jill
Legal and Business: PolyGram Filmed Entertainment and International Distribution. Partner Kuhn & Co. Ltd.

Tartikof, Brandon
Onetime Head of NBC.

Tauber, Jim
President/MD of Propaganda Films (1992). Reported to Steve Golin and Sigurjon Sighvatsson. Now with Steve Golin's new company, Anonymous.

Tennant, Bill
Sometime President of Casablanca Filmworks and MD of VVL – PolyGram UK's specialist video company.

Till, Stewart
President of PFE International. Founder of Signpost Films.

Timmer, Jan
President of PolyGram. Moved to Philips as President in 1990 until his retirement on 1st October, 1996.

Wasserman, Lew
Legendary Head of MCA.

Weinstein, Harvey
Co-founder of Miramax.

Weinstein, Bob
Co-founder of Miramax.

Wells, Frank
Legendary Hollywood lawyer and executive. No. 2 to Michael Eisner. Killed in a helicopter crash.

Woolley, Stephen
Palace Productions. Went on to form Company of Wolves with Neil Jordan.

2
PolyGram Filmed Entertainment chronology

Pre-1991

- Conducted discreet production activities as part of trial period before the development of a formal business plan. Progressively acquired more control over the distribution of the titles.

- Produced low cost films and pre-sold world-wide rights to third parties.

- Established Manifesto Film Sales for foreign sales.

- Acquired an interest in Propaganda Films and Working Title Films.

- Experienced early success with release of *Wild at Heart* which won the Palme d'Or at the 1990 Cannes Film Festival.

1991

- Received approval for business plan from PolyGram Board of Directors.

1992

- Initiated implementation of film business plan.

- Established Los Angeles operations headquarters (managed by Michael Kuhn) and international headquarters in London (managed by Stewart Till).

- Commenced production of films principally through Working Title Films, Propaganda Films, A&M Films and Interscope Communications.

- Acquired remaining interests in Propaganda Films.

- Established Gramercy Pictures in 50/50 partnership with Universal for speciality domestic film distribution.

- Acquired interest in Interscope Communications.

- Established distribution operations in the UK and France.

- Initial plan consisted of producing or acquiring 8-15 films per year with US rights to big budget films pre-sold to the major studios and the smaller budget films distributed domestically through Gramercy Pictures.

- International territories were pre-sold to third parties through Manifesto Film Sales.

1993

- Acquired Movies Film Productions BV, a Dutch independent film producer and distributor.

- Acquired Pan Europeanne, a French independent theatrical distributor.

- Acquired remaining interest in Working Title Films.

1994

- Acquired the catalogue and film production facilities of Island World, which included the Island and Atlantic film catalogues.

- Established a joint venture with Sogepaq Distribution in Spain.

- Entered into first off-balance sheet film lease transaction of $200 million.

1995

- Purchased ITC catalogue. Acquisition formed the basis of PolyGram Television.

- Established Canadian distribution operations.

- Acquired the distribution operations of Independent Films, a Belgium theatrical distributor and film producer.

1996

- Acquired remaining interest in Interscope Communications.

- Began distributing all Interscope films upon expiration of Interscope's output deal with Disney.

- Acquired the remaining 50 per cent of Gramercy Pictures from Universal.

- Established distribution operations in Australia.

- Became an initial shareholder in Sundance Channel LLC, a joint venture with Sundance Television and Show Time Networks Inc., a subsidiary of Viacom, Inc.

- Entered into second off-balance sheet film lease transaction of $300 million.

1997

- Announced the formation of US distribution arm, PolyGram Films to distribute larger budget, commercially driven films in the US.

- Officially formed PolyGram Television.

- Established German and Austrian distribution operations.

- Acquired Swiss independent distributor Monopole Pathe Films.

1998

- Acquired the Epic film catalogue.

- Entered into a joint venture with Warner Bros. to co-finance and distribute Castle Rock films.

- Together with Warner Bros. arranged a $200 million off-balance sheet facility to fund Castle Rock films.

- Received commitment from major global lender for off-balance sheet financing for Reitman/Pollock produced films.

- Negotiated financing vehicle from consortium of banks for $650 million securitisation to finance acquisition of completed films (not finalised).

- Established Italian distribution operations.

Future

- Plan to establish direct distribution operations in Latin America – Brazil (operational 1/99) and Mexico (operational 1/00).

3
Timeline

1977-79

Casablanca Filmworks (Casablanca Records bought by PolyGram). Headed by Neil Bogart and Peter Guber

---

The Deep (1977), *Midnight Express* (1978), *Thank God, It's Friday* (1978), *Agatha* (1979)

1980

Bogart forced to resign and Gordon Stulberg brought in as CEO. Jon Peters joins. PolyGram Pictures established in March, PolyGram Television in October

---

Foxes (with Jodie Foster)

1981

King of the Mountain (Universal), *Endless Love* (Universal), *Deadly Blessing* (UA), *An American Werewolf in London* (Universal), *Pursuit of DB Cooper*

1982

PolyGram Pictures collapses

Kuhn co-founds PolyGram Music Video

Split Image (Orion), *Six Weeks* (Universal)

1986

Michael Kuhn gears up interest in film and becomes involved with Propaganda

P.I. Private Investigations

1987

5 Jan: Malcolm Ritchie joins PolyGram International

11 Dec: 49 per cent of Propaganda Films (effective 5 Jan 88): $3.25m

The Blue Iguana

1988

Jan: New Business Division moves to offices in 30 Berkeley Square (6th floor)

March: First meeting with Working Title Films. Establishment of WTTV Ltd. (Ritchie director): tv movies

Sept: Proposed buy-out of MGM/UA Communications

Fear Anxiety and Depression

1989

Manifesto Film Sales established

Working Title Films (49%)

PolyGram Filmproduktions established

PolyGram goes public

1 Aug: PolyGram purchases Island Records

Chicago Joe and the Showgirl, Daddy's Dyin... Who's Got the Will? Fools of Fortune, Kill Me Again, A Row of Crows

1990

12 Feb: PolyGram passes on Oak Films (TV production and distribution)

May: A&M Films acquired (approved 14 Sep 1989)

16-18 May: Cannes: *Wild at Heart* wins Palme D'Or

5-8 Sept: Michael Kuhn and Malcolm Ritchie meet in New York with Harvey and Bob Weinstein of Miramax Films to discuss proposed purchase of interest in Miramax

11-20 Nov: LA MGM (Kirk Kerkorian)

Dakota Road, Drop Dead Fred, Rubin and Ed, Wild at Heart

1991

Jan: David Fine leaves PolyGram: new president, Alain Lévy

Jan: Meetings with Palace Pictures ($2m) – Palace collapses (cf. *The Egos have Landed*)
London Independent Broadcasting (PolyGram, Working Title, Palace, Menthorn): tv franchise bid – lost to LWT

16-21 May:Cannes: *Barton Fink* wins Palme D'Or

14 Aug: Kuhn and Ritchie present 'PolyGram & Films' to Philips Board in Eindhoven

Sept: Buy-out of Propaganda (March 1992) and Working Title (Jan 1992)

2 Dec: Nelson Entertainment's Show Time (pay TV)/Viacom (syndication) pay TV slots

Barton Fink, Candyman, Edward II, Indecent Woman, London Kills Me, Man and Two Women, A Midnight Clear, Red Rock West, Robin Hood, Ruby (Lovefield), A Stranger Among Us, Truth or Dare, In Bed With Madonna

1992

PolyGram Filmed Entertainment established

Jan 1:   100 per cent Working Title acquisition. Stewart Till appointed president of the International Division of PFE

Jan: Rumours of PolyGram taking over struggling Orion Pictures unfounded

15 Feb: Malcolm Ritchie moves to LA

Feb: PFE offices in Maple Drive, Beverly Hills (sublet from Sinclair Tenenbaum, LA lawyers)

March: *Ruby* released

March: 100 per cent Propaganda acquisition

29 April: LA riots (Rodney King)

May: Palace/Scala deal

Egg Pictures output deal

May: Gramercy Pictures (Schwartz begins on 1 June)

Columbia (Sony) large film and video (Columbia TriStar) distribution deal

31 Aug: PFE presentation to Group Management Committee

2 Oct: 51 per cent Interscope deal closed

28 Oct: 1st screening of *Kalifornia* (first 100 per cent PFE film)

Nov: Proposed acquisition of Video Vision Ltd. (formerly Virgin Vision Ltd.)

Bob Roberts, Close to Eden, Gun in Betty Lou's Handbag, Lights Out, Map of the Human Heart, Un Coeur en Hiver

1993

18 Jan:	Gramercy move into offices in Alden Drive with Working Title LA
22 Jan:	Viacom agreements
30 May-5 Jun:	PolyGram MD conference in Miami
Sep:	Island Film's integration into PFE
	$200 m. lease deal to allow off-balance sheet financing
Dec:	PFE moves to the Ice House (Civic Centre Drive)

Ballad of Little Jo, The Cutting Edge, Dangerous Woman, Dazed and Confused, Home of Our Own, A House of Cards, Kalifornia, King of the Hill, Lake Consequence, Posse, Tango, The Young Americans

---

1994

Jan:	Manifesto Film Sales to be renamed PolyGram Film International
Jan:	MFP/Meteor (Benelux distribution)
Jan:	Pan Europeenne (French distribution)
22-26 May:	PolyGram International Convention (Vancouver)
1 July:	Island Pictures acquisition
Sept:	Sogepaq (Spanish distribution)
	Entered into first off-balance sheet film lease transaction of $200 million
16 Sept:	ITC catalogue acquisition approved by Fine ($162 m)

Adventures of Priscilla, Queen of the Desert, The Air Up There, The Away From Home, Before the Rain, Dead Connection, Dream Lover, Foreign Student, Four Weddings and A Funeral, Gnome Named Gnorm, Holy Matrimony, The Hudsucker Proxy, Jason's Lyric, Nell, Romeo is Bleeding, Room Mates, Savage Nights, SFW, Shallow Grave, Terminal Velocity, U.F.O.

1995

1 Jan: Acquisition of ITC Entertainment Group's film and TV catalogue

Jan 19-25: Sundance (Gramercy), Park City, Utah

Canadian distribution

Acquisition of distribution operations of Independent Films (Belgium)

April: Acquires two MTV channels in Asia

Sept: PFE Australia (distribution)

Sept: Possible acquisition of Samuel Goldwyn Co. by PFE

Deal with MGM for theatrical distribution (PFE to retain video rights)

Robert Cort leaves Interscope

Oct: $400m deal with Viacom's Show Time Networks Inc. for PFE product

---

Canadian Bacon, Candyman 2, Carrington, Dead Man Walking, French Kiss, Halcyon Days, Home for the Holidays, Jack and Sarah, Jumanji, Loch Ness, Moonlight and Valentino, Operation Dumbo Drop, Panther, A Pig's Tale, Summer Camp, Shooter, Tie That Binds, The Usual Suspects

1996

PolyGram buys out Gramercy

End of Interscope's Disney output deal: PFE to distribute

PolyGram establishes European Film Companies Alliance (EFCA)

Jan 18-28: Sundance (Gramercy)

Michael Kuhn joins Sundance Board of Trustees/deal with Sundance Channel

March: 'Project Star' – PolyGram attempt to bid for MGM

**26 April –
3 May:** PolyGram MD conference in Hong Kong

May: Zane Devine appointed a Senior VP at PFE

6 June: Foster sues PolyGram & Propaganda re: *The Game*

2nd off-balance sheet film lease transaction of $300 million

June: MGM bid fails (management bid by Kirk Kerkorian and Mancuso successful)

2 Dec: Malcolm Ritchie COO of PFE in London

The Associate, Barb Wire, Bound, Eddie, Fargo, Garcu, Le Haine, Le Huitieme Jour, Jude, Kazaam, Little Death, Mr. Holland's Opus, Mr. Reliable, Mulholland Falls, Portrait of a Lady, Le Ridicule, Sleepers, A Thousand Acres, Trainspotting, Two Much, When We Were Kings

1997

Jan: PFE Germany (distribution) and Austria

3 March: Fundraising 'bash' for Sundance Institute

March: Bob Sanitsky (ICM) heads up PolyGram TV

2 May: Launch of US distribution outfit, PolyGram Films (aka PolyGram Filmed Entertainment Distribution)

24-30 May: PolyGram MD conference in New Orleans

Possible takeover of Golden Harvest discussed

Interest in acquiring Television label/developing TV production

April-June: Michael Kuhn seeks support for European Guarantee Fund prior to meeting of European Council of Culture on 30th of June

Sept: *Bean* a massive success in pre-US release

3 Nov: First meeting of the EC High Level Group on Audiovisual Policy

2 Dec: PolyGram acquires Epic Library (1045 titles) owned by French Government agency, CDR ($225 m)

31 Dec: Island shuts down

American Werewolf in Paris, Bean, The Borrowers, The Game, The Gingerbread Man, Gridlock'd, How to be a Player, A Life Less Ordinary, The Matchmaker, Photographing Fairies, The Relic, Snow White, Spice World

1998

Early	PFE Italy (distribution)
Early	PFE Switzerland (distribution)
	$200 million off-balance sheet facility to fund Castle Rock Films with Warner Bros
2 March:	Sundance Institute benefit dinner at the Kuhns' home
6 April:	Michael Kuhn addresses European Commission on Audiovisual Policy in Birmingham
May:	Bevan and Fellner honoured as producers at Cannes
7 May:	Philips announces intention to sell 75 per cent share in PolyGram
May:	Possible interest in PolyGram by Ovitz (and others). Rumours of management buy-out
22 May:	Philips to accept Seagram's bid for PolyGram
21 June:	PolyGram Supervisory Board Meeting
22 June:	Alain Lévy resigns
June:	Michael Kuhn prepares Information Memorandum for prospective PFE buyers
14 July:	Chris McGurk elected president of Universal Pictures, two years after joining
August:	Various bids are made for PFE
21 Oct:	MGM agrees to buy PFE's library from Seagram ($250 m)
Nov:	Cor Boonstra's estranged wife kidnapped
16 Nov:	Frank Biondi fired
19 Nov:	Canal Plus unable to purchase PFE's international distribution operation due to Seagram's high asking price
25 Nov:	Extraordinary Meeting of PolyGram Shareholders, Baarn

9 Dec: Jan Cook retires

10 Dec: Kuhn's departure announced

Dec: Universal speculates that it will merge Gramercy with October Films

11 Dec: Seagram takeover of PolyGram complete ($10.4 billion). No buyer for PFE – to be merged with Universal

---

Barney's Great Adventure, The Big Lebowski, Elizabeth, Hard Rain, Hi-Lo Country, The Land Girls, Lock, Stock and Two Smoking Barrels, Return to Paradise, Very Bad Things, What Dreams May Come, Your Friends and Neighbours

1999

15 Feb: PFE Management Presentation suggesting continuation of international distribution (Stewart Till)

Being John Malkovich, The Green Mile, Notting Hill, Plunkett and MacCleane, Waking the Dead, Wonderland

2000

20 June: Vivendi announces merger/buy-out of Seagram for $30/34 billion. The company will become Vivendi Universal

---

Nurse Betty

4
PolyGram Filmed Entertainment: Film List

Film	Production	Release	Distribution
Adventures of Priscilla, Queen of the Desert, The	AFFC/Michael Hamlyn and Al Clarke	1994	
Air Up There, The	Interscope	1994	
American Werewolf in London, An	Universal	1981	
Associate, The	Interscope	1996	
Backbeat	Palace/Scala	1993	Gramercy
Ballad of Little Jo, The	Joco	1993	Manifesto
Barb Wire	Propaganda	1996	
Barney's Great Adventure	Lyrick Studios	1998	
Barton Fink	Circle	1991	Manifesto
Bean	Working Title	1997	
Before the Rain/Pred Dozhdot	Noe	1994	
Being John Malkovich	Propaganda	1999	
Big Lebowski, The	Working Title	1998	
Blue Iguana, The	Propaganda	1987	
Bob Roberts	Propaganda	1992	Manifesto
Borrowers, The	Working Title	1997	
Bound	Gramercy/Spelling/ De Laurentiis	1996	Gramercy
Boys	Interscope	1996	
Canadian Bacon	Propaganda	1995	
Candyman	Propaganda	1991	
Candyman 2: Farewell to the Flesh	Propaganda	1995	

Film	Production	Release	Distribution
Carrington	Cinéa	1995	Gramercy
Chicago Joe and the Showgirl	Working Title	1989	Manifesto
Close to Eden	Propaganda	1992	Manifesto
Cutting Edge	Interscope	1993	
Dad Savage	Rob Jones/ Sweet Child Films	1998	
Daddy's Dyin'...Who's Got the Will?	Propaganda	1989	Manifesto
Dakota Road	Working Title	1990	Manifesto
Dangerous Woman	Gramercy	1993	Gramercy
Dead Connection	Propaganda	1994	
Dead Man Walking	Working Title/ Havoc Inc.	1995	
Deadly Blessing	UA	1981	
Dream Lover	Propaganda	1994	Manifesto/Gramercy
Drop Dead Fred	Working Title	1990	Manifesto
Eddie	Island	1996	
Edward II	Working Title	1991	
Elizabeth	Working Title	1998	
Endless Love	Universal	1981	
Fargo	Working Title	1996	
Fear, Anxiety and Depression	Propaganda	1988	
Fools of Fortune	Working Title	1989	Manifesto
Force Majeure	CAPAC	1989	
Foreign Student	Universal	1994	Gramercy
Four Weddings and a Funeral	Working Title	1994	Gramercy
French Kiss/Paris Match	Working Title	1995	
Game, The	Propaganda	1997	
Garcu, Le	France 2 Cinéma	1996	Gramercy
Gingerbread Man, The	Island	1997	PolyGram Films
Giorgino	Heathcliff	1994	
Gnome Named Gnorm, A	Interscope	1994	

Film	Production	Release	Distribution
Good Man in Africa, A	Universal	1994	Gramercy
Green Mile, The	Warner Bros	1999	
Gridlock'd	Def/Interscope/Dragon	1997	
Gun in Betty Lou's Handbag	Interscope	1992	
Guy	Pandora	1996	
Haine, La	Gramercy	1996	Gramercy
Halcyon Days/Towards Zero/ Innocent Lies	Cinéa	1995	Manifesto
Hard Rain	PFE	1998	
Hi-Lo Country, The	Working Title	1998	
Holy Matrimony	Interscope	1994	
Home for the Holidays	Egg	1995	
Home of Our Own, A	A&M	1993	Manifesto/Gramercy
House of Cards	A&M	1993	
How to be a Player	Island/Def/Outlaw	1997	
Hudsucker Proxy, The	Working Title/Silver	1994	
Huitieme Jour, Le	Cinéa/D.A. Films	1996	Gramercy
Indecent Woman	Meteor Film Production	1991	
Jack and Sarah	Gramercy/Canal Plus	1995	Gramercy
Jason's Lyric	Propaganda	1994	
Johnsons, De	Meteor Film Production	1992	
Jude	Revolution	1996	
Jumanji	Interscope	1995	
Kalifornia Manifesto/Gramercy	Propaganda	1993	
Kazaam	Interscope	1996	
Keys to Tulsa	ITC/Empire	1997	
Kill Me Again	Propaganda	1989	
King of the Hill	Universal	1993	Gramercy
King of the Mountain	Universal	1981	
Lake Consequence	Zalman King	1993	Manifesto

Film	Production	Release	Distribution
Land and Freedom	PFE	1995	Gramercy
Land Girls, The	C4/Intermedia	1998	
Life Less Ordinary, A	C4/Figment	1997	
Lights Out	Propaganda	1992	Manifesto
Little Death, The	Island	1996	
Loch Ness	Working Title	1995	
Lock, Stock and Two Smoking Barrels	PFE	1998	PFE/Gramercy
London Kills Me	Working Title	1991	Manifesto
Man and Two Women, A/ Homme te Deux Femmes, Un	Films A2	1991	Manifesto
Map of the Human Heart	Working Title	1992	Manifesto/Miramax
Matchmaker, The	Working Title	1997	
Menace	Island	1996	
Midnight Clear	A&M	1991	
Midnight Express	Casablanca Filmworks	1978	Columbia
Moonlight and Valentino	Working Title	1995	
Mr. Holland's Opus	Interscope	1996	
Mr. Reliable	Specific Films	1996	Gramercy
Mulholland Falls	PFE	1996	
Nell	Egg	1994	
New Jersey Drive	Gramercy/ 40 Acres and a Mule	1995	Gramercy
No Looking Back	Good Machine	1998	
Notting Hill	Working Title	1999	
Nurse Betty	Propaganda	2000	
Operation Dumbo Drop	Interscope	1995	
P.I. Private Investigations	Propaganda	1986	
Panther	Working Title	1995	
Paws	Hamlyn	1997	
Photographing Fairies	PFE	1997	

Film	Production	Release	Distribution
Pig's Tale, A/Summer Camp	Propaganda	1995	
Plunkett and MacCleane	Working Title	1999	Gramercy
Portrait of a Lady, The	Propaganda	1996	
Posse	Working Title	1993	Manifesto/Gramercy
Proposition, The	Interscope	1998	
Pursuit of DB Cooper	PFE	1981	Universal
Red Rock West	Propaganda	1991	
Relic, The	PFE	1997	
Return to Paradise	PFE	1998	
Ridicule	Cinéa	1996	
Road Dogs	Universal	1994	Gramercy
Robin Hood	Working Title	1991	
Romeo is Bleeding	Working Title	1994	Maniseto/Gramercy
Room Mates	Interscope	1994	
Row of Crows, A	Propaganda	1989	
Rubin and Ed	Working Title	1990	
Ruby (Lovefield)	Propaganda	1991	Manifesto
Savage Nights	UGC Pan-Europeanne	1994	Gramercy
SFW	Propaganda	1994	
Shallow Grave	C4/Gramercy	1994	Gramercy
Shooter, The/Hidden Assassin	Canal Plus	1995	
Sleepers	Propaganda	1996	
Snow White	Interscope	1997	
Spice World	PFE	1997	
Split Image	Orion	1982	
Stranger Among Us, A	Propaganda	1991	Manifesto
Tango	Cinéa	1993	
Terminal Velocity	Interscope	1994	
Thousand Acres, A	Propaganda	1996	
Tie That Binds, The	Interscope	1995	
Trainspotting	C4/Figment	1996	

Film	Production	Release	Distribution
Truth or Dare/ In Bed With Madonna	Propaganda	1991	
Two Much	Interscope	1996	
U.F.O.	PFE	1994	
Un Coeur en Hiver	Cinéa	1992	
Unveiled	PFE	1994	
Usual Suspects, The	Gramercy	1995	Gramercy
Very Bad Things	Interscope	1998	PFE
Waking the Dead	Egg	1999	
What Becomes of the Broken Hearted?	PFE	1999	Gramercy
What Dreams May Come	Interscope	1998	
When We Were Kings	PFE	1996	
Whiskey Down/Just Your Luck	Propaganda	1996	PolyGram Video
Wild at Heart	Propaganda	1990	Manifesto
Wonderland	Revolution	1999	
Young Americans, The	Working Title	1993	Manifesto
Your Friends and Neighbours	Gramercy	1998	Gramercy

5
Film credits

Title	Year	Director	Writing Credits	Produced by
Adventures of Priscilla, Queen of the Desert, The	1994	Stephan Elliott	Stephan Elliott	Al Clark Michael Hamlyn Rebel Russell (executive) Sue Seeary (associate)
Agatha	1979	Michael Apted	Kathleen Tynan (story)	
Air Up There, The	1994	Paul Michael Glaser	Max Apple (written by)	
American Werewolf in London, An	1981	John Landis	John Landis	George Folsey Jr. Peter Guber (executive) Jon Peters (executive)
Associate, The	1996	Donald Petrie	Jenaro Prieto (novel El Socio) Jean-Claude Carrire (screenplay L'Associ) Ren Gainville (screenplay L'Associ) Nick Thiel (screenplay)	Robert W. Cort (executive) Ted Field (executive) Ren Gainville (co-producer) Frederic Golchan Michael A. Helfant (co-producer) Scott Kroopf (executive) Adam Leipzig David Madden (executive) Patrick Markey
Backbeat	1993	Iain Softley	Iain Softley Michael Thomas Stephen Ward	Paul Cowan (line) Sarah Curtis (co-producer) Finola Dwyer Hanno Huth (executive) Nik Powell (executive) Stephen M. Williams (co-producer) Stephen Woolley
Ballad of Little Jo, The	1993	Maggie Greenwald	Maggie Greenwald (written by)	Fred Berner Ira Deutchman (executive) Anne Dillon (associate) Brenda Goodman John Sloss (executive)
Barb Wire	1996	David Hogan	Chris Warner (characters in comic) Ilene Chaiken (story) Chuck Pfarrer (screenplay) Ilene Chaiken (screenplay)	Dennis Brody (associate) Robert Del Valle (line) Peter Heller (executive) Ray Manzella (associate) Todd Moyer Mike Richardson Brad Wyman
Barney's Great Adventure	1998	Steve Gomer	Stephen White (story) Sheryl Leach (story) Dennis DeShazer (story) Stephen White	Martha Chang (co-executive) Dennis DeShazer Sheryl Leach Ben Myron (executive) Jim Rowley (co-producer)
Barton Fink	1991	Joel Coen	Ethan Coen Joel Coen	Ben Barenholtz (executive) Ethan Coen Bill Durkin (executive) Jim Pedas (executive) Ted Pedas (executive) Graham Place

Cinematograhy	Film Editing	Special Effects	Production Design	Costume Design	Cast includes
Brian J. Breheny	Sue Blainey		Owen Paterson	Tim Chappel Lizzy Gardiner	Hugo Weaving Guy Pearce Terence Stamp Bill Hunter
					Dustin Hoffman Vanessa Redgrave Timothy Dalton Helen Morse
					Kevin Bacon Charles Gitonga Maina Yolanda Vazquez Winston Ntshona
Robert Paynter	Malcolm Campbell	Martin Gutteridge Garth Inns		Deborah Nadoolman	Joe Belcher David Naughton Griffin Dunne David Schofield
Alex Nepomniaschy	Bonnie Koehler	Greg Cannom	Andrew Jackness	April Ferry	Whoopi Goldberg Dianne Wiest Eli Wallach Timothy Daly
Ian Wilson	Martin Walsh		Joseph Bennett	Sheena Napier	Marcelle Duprey Stephen Dorff Ian Hart John White
Declan Quinn	Keith Reamer		Mark Friedberg	Claudia Brown	Suzy Amis Bo Hopkins Ian McKellen David Chung
Rick Bota Michael A. Jones	Peter Schink	Don Gray John E. Gray Roland Loew Eric Roberts	Jean-Philippe Carp	Rosanna Norton	Pamela Anderson Temuera Morrison Victoria Rowell Jack Noseworthy
Sandi Sissel	Richard Halsey	Max W. Anderson Edward Svetlik Simon Webb	Vincent Jefferds		George Hearn Shirley Douglas Trevor Morgan Diana Rice
Roger Deakins	Ethan Coen (as Roderick Jaynes) Joel Coen (as Roderick Jaynes)	Guy Himber Laurel Schneider Robert Spurlock	Dennis Gassner	Richard Hornung	John Turturro John Goodman Judy Davis Michael Lerner

Title	Year	Director	Writing Credits	Produced by
Batman	1989	Tim Burton	Bob Kane (Batman characters) Sam Hamm (story) Sam Hamm (screenplay) Warren Skaaren (screenplay)	Peter Guber Barbara Kalish (associate) Chris Kenny (co-producer) Benjamin Melniker (executive) Jon Peters Michael E. Uslan (executive)
Bean	1997	Mel Smith	Richard Curtis Robin Driscoll	Rowan Atkinson (executive) Peter Bennet-Jones Tim Bevan Richard Curtis (executive) Eric Fellner Rebecca O'Brien (co-producer)
Being John Malkovich	1999	Spike Jonze	Charlie Kaufman (written by)	Steve Golin Charlie Kaufman (executive) Michael Kuhn (executive) Vincent Landay Sandy Stern Michael Stipe
Big Lebowski, The	1998	Joel Coen	Ethan Coen (written by) Joel Coen (written by)	Tim Bevan (executive) John Cameron (co-producer) Ethan Coen Eric Fellner (executive)
Blue Iguana, The	1988	John Lafia	John Lafia	Winnie Fredriksz (associate) Steve Golin Alejandra HernÆndez Esquivel (line) Michael Kuhn (executive) Angel Flores Marini (co-producer) Othon Roffiel (co-producer) Sigurjon Sighvatsson Nigel Sinclair (executive)
Bob Roberts	1992	Tim Robbins	Tim Robbins	Tim Bevan (executive) James Bigwood (associate) Forrest Murray Allan F. Nicholls (associate) Ronna B. Wallace (executive) Paul Webster (executive)
Borrowers, The	1997	Peter Hewitt	Mary Norton (novels) Gavin Scott (screenplay) John Kamps (screenplay)	Tim Bevan Liza Chasin (co-producer) Eric Fellner Debra Hayward (co-producer) Mary Richards (line) Rachel Talalay Walt deFaria (executive)
Boys	1996	Stacy Cochran	Stacy Cochran	Robert W. Cort (executive) Paul Feldsher Ted Field (executive) Peter Frankfurt Erica Huggins Scott Kroopf (executive) Rudd Simmons (co-producer)

Cinematograhy	Film Editing	Special Effects	Production Design	Costume Design	Cast includes
Roger Pratt	Ray Lovejoy	Steve Crawley John Evans	Anton Furst	Linda Henrikson Bob Ringwood	Michael Keaton Jack Nicholson Kim Basinger Robert Wuhl
Francis Kenny	Chris Blunden		Peter S. Larkin	Hope Hanafin	Rowan Atkinson Peter MacNicol John Mills Pamela Reed
Lance Acord	Eric Zumbrunnen	Ryan Arndt Lori Freitag-Hild John E. Gray Bryan Grill John Ziegler	K.K. Barrett	Casey Storm	John Cusack Cameron Diaz Ned Bellamy Eric Weinstein
Roger Deakins	Ethan Coen (as Roderick Jaynes) Joel Coen (as Roderick Jaynes) Tricia Cooke	Rick Bongiovanni Tom Chesney Roderic 'Mick' Duff	Rick Heinrichs	Mary Zophres	Jeff Bridges John Goodman Julianne Moore Steve Buscemi
Rodolfo SÆnchez	Scott Chestnut	Benjamn Bentez Guillermo Bonilla Jorge Farfan Rosina Farfan Enrique Gmez Lara	Cynthia Sowder	Isis Mussenden	Dylan McDermott Jessica Harper James Russo Pamela Gidley
Jean Lpine	Lisa Zeno Churgin	John Alagua Steidl Balzer Michael Ventresco	Richard Hoover	Bridget Kelly	Tim Robbins Giancarlo Esposito Alan Rickman Ray Wise
Trevor Brooker John Fenner	David Freeman	Digby Milner	Gemma Jackson	Marie France	John Goodman Jim Broadbent Mark Williams Celia Imrie
Robert Elswit	Camilla Toniolo	Matthew Vogel	Dan Bishop	Lucy W. Corrigan	Winona Ryder Lukas Haas John C. Reilly James LeGros

Title	Year	Director	Writing Credits	Produced by
Canadian Bacon	1995	Michael Moore	Michael Moore (written by)	Stuart M. Besser (line) David Brown Freddy De Mann (executive) Louis G. Friedman (line) Kathleen Glynn (co-producer) Terry Miller (associate) Michael Moore Ron Rotholz Sigurjon Sighvatsson (executive)
Candyman	1992	Bernard Rose	Clive Barker (story The Forbidden) Bernard Rose	Clive Barker (executive) Steve Golin Gregory Goodman (line) Alan Poul Sigurjon Sighvatsson
Candyman: Farewell to the Flesh	1995	Bill Condon	Clive Barker (story) Rand Ravich (screenplay) Mark Kruger (screenplay)	Clive Barker (executive) Tim Clawson (supervising) Gregg Fienberg (as Gregg D. Fienberg) Anna C. Miller (associate) Sigurjon Sighvatsson
Carrington	1995	Christopher Hampton	Christopher Hampton Michael Holroyd (book)	Francis Boespflug (executive) Philippe Carcassonne (executive) John McGrath Ronald Shedlo Chris Thompson (associate) Fabienne Vonier (executive)
Chicago Joe and the Showgirl	1990	Bernard Rose	David Yallop	Tim Bevan Jane Frazer (associate)
Climate for Killing, A aka A Row of Crows	1991	J.S. Cardone	J.S. Cardone (written by)	
Cutting Edge, The	1992	Paul Michael Glaser	Tony Gilroy (written by)	Robert W. Cort Ted Field Karen Murphy Dean O'Brien (co-producer) Cynthia Sherman (co-producer)
Dad Savage	1998	Betsan Morris Evans	Steve Williams	Robert Jones Gwynneth Lloyd Paul Sarony (line)
Daddy's Dyin'... Who's Got the Will?	1990	Jack Fisk	Del Shores (play) Del Shores (screenplay)	Dennis Bishop (line) Steve Golin Michael Kuhn (executive) Monty Montgomery Jay Roewe Sigurjon Sighvatsson Nigel Sinclair (executive)
Dakota Road	1990	Nick Ward	Nick Ward	Donna Grey Sarah Radclyffe (executive)
Dangerous Woman, A	1993	Stephen Gyllenhaal	Mary McGarry Morris (novel) Naomi Foner (screenplay)	Naomi Foner Kathleen Kennedy (executive) Steven Spielberg (executive) (uncredited) Patricia Whitcher (line)

Cinematograhy	Film Editing	Special Effects	Production Design	Costume Design	Cast includes
Haskell Wexler	Michael Berenbaum Wendy Stanzler	Bob Hall Arthur Langevin	Carol Spier	Kathleen Glynn	John Candy Alan Alda Rhea Perlman Kevin Pollak.
Anthony B. Richmond	Dan Rae	Martin Bresin Dale Ettema Steven Carlton Ficke Don Hasting Jeffrey Knott Brian Latt Scott Sand	Jane Ann Stewart	Leonard Pollack	Virginia Madsen Tony Todd Xander Berkeley Kasi Lemmons
Tobias A. Schliessler	Virginia Katz	John C. Hartigan	Barry Robison	Bruce Finlayson	Tony Todd Kelly Rowan William O'Leary Bill Nunn
Denis Lenoir	George Akers		Caroline Amies	Penny Rose	Emma Thompson Jonathan Pryce Steven Waddington Samuel West
Mike Southon	Dan Rae		Gemma Jackson	Bob Ringwood	John Lahr Emily Lloyd Liz Fraser Kiefer Sutherland
Michael Cardone					John Beck Katharine Ross Steven Bauer Mia Sara
Jon Cassar Elliot Davis	Michael E. Polakow	Jason Board Arthur Langevin	David Gropman	William Ivey Long	D.B. Sweeney Moira Kelly Roy Dotrice Terry O'Quinn
Gavin Finney	Guy Bensley		Michael Carlin	Rachael Fleming	Patrick Stewart Kevin McKidd Helen McCrory Joseph McFadden
Paul Elliott	Edward A. Warschilka				Beau Bridges Beverly D'Angelo Tess Harper Judge Reinhold
Ian Wilson	William Diver		Careen Hertzog	Careen Hertzog	David Bamber Amelda Brown Jason Carter Charlotte Chatton
Robert Elswit	Angelo Corrao Harvey Rosenstock	Larry Fioritto	David Brisbin	Susie DeSanto	Debra Winger Laurie Metcalf Barbara Hershey John Terry

Title	Year	Director	Writing Credits	Produced by
Dazed and Confused	1993	Richard Linklater	Richard Linklater (written by)	Sean Daniel James Jacks Richard Linklater Anne Walker-McBay (co-producer)
Dead Connection	1994	Nigel Dick	Jonathan Tydor (story) Larry Golin	Gregg Fienberg Steve Golin Gregory Goodman (line) Gary Milkis (executive) Johanna Ray (associate) Sigurjon Sighvatsson (executive) Lynn Weimer (associate)
Dead Man Walking	1995	Tim Robbins	Helen Prejean (book Dead Man Walking) Tim Robbins	Tim Bevan (executive) Eric Fellner (executive) Jon Kilik Allan F. Nicholls (associate) (as Allan Nicholls) Tim Robbins Mark Seldis (associate) Rudd Simmons Bob White (associate)
Deadly Blessing	1981	Wes Craven	Glenn M. Benest (story) Matthew Barr (story) Glenn M. Benest (screenplay) Matthew Barr (screenplay) Wes Craven (screenplay)	Matthew Barr (associate) Glenn M. Benest (associate) William S. Gilmore (executive) (as William Gilmore) Patricia S. Herskovic Max A. Keller Micheline H. Keller
Deep, The	1977	Peter Yates	Peter Benchley (also novel) Tracy Keenan Wynn	Peter Guber George Justin (associate)
Dream Lover	1994	Nicholas Kazan	Nicholas Kazan (written by)	Elon Dershowitz (co-producer) Louis G. Friedman (line) Tim Glawson (supervising) Steve Golin (executive) Lauren Lloyd Wallis Nicita Edward R. Pressman (executive) Sigurjon Sighvatsson
Drop Dead Fred	1991	Ate de Jong	Carlos Davis Anthony Fingleton	Paul Webster
Eddie	1996	Steve Rash	Steve Zacharias (story) Jeff Buhai (story) Jon Connolly (story) David Loucka (story) Jon Connolly (screenplay) David Loucka (screenplay) Eric Champnella (screenplay) Keith Coogan (screenplay) Steve Zacharias (screenplay) Jeff Buhai (screenplay)	Ronald M. Bozman (executive) (as Ron Bozman) Jeff Buhai (executive) Mark Burg Andrew Gunn (co-producer) David Permut Steve Zacharias (executive)
Edward II	1991)	Derek Jarman	Ken Butler Steve Clark-Hall Derek Jarman Christopher Marlowe (play) Stephen McBride Antony Root	Steve Clark-Hall

Cinematograhy	Film Editing	Special Effects	Production Design	Costume Design	Cast includes
Lee Daniel	Sandra Adair		John Frick	Katherine Dover	Jason London Joey Lauren Adams Milla Jovovich Shawn Andrews
David Bridges	Jonathan P. Shaw	Martin Bresin Mike Schorr Thomas E. Surprenant	Jon Gary Steele	Alexandra Welker	Michael Madsen Lisa Sinclair Paul Leslie Disley Simon Kenny
Roger Deakins	Lisa Zeno Churgin Ray Hubley		Richard Hoover	Renee Ehrlich Kalfus	Susan Sarandon Sean Penn Robert Prosky Raymond J. Barry.
Robert C. Jessup	Richard Bracken	Jack Bennett	Jack Marty	Patricia McKiernan	Maren Jensen Sharon Stone Susan Buckner Jeff East
Christopher Challis	David Berlatsky	Ira Anderson Jr	Anthony Masters	Ron Talsky	Jacqueline Bisset Nick Nolte Dick Anthony Williams Robert Shaw
Jean-Yves Escoffier	Susan R. Crutcher Jill Savitt	Michael Schorr	Richard Hoover	Barbara Tfank	James Spader Mdchen Amick Fredric Lehne Bess Armstrong
Peter Deming	Marshall Harvey	Brian Griffin		Carol Wood	Phoebe Cates Rik Mayall Marsha Mason Tim Matheson
Victor J. Kemper	Richard Halsey		Dan Davis	Molly Maginnis	Whoopi Goldberg Frank Langella Dennis Farina Richard Jenkins
Ian Wilson	George Akers		Christopher Hobbs	Sandy Powell	

Title	Year	Director	Writing Credits	Produced by
Elizabeth	1998	Shekhar Kapur	Michael Hirst	Tim Bevan Liza Chasin (co-producer) Eric Fellner Debra Hayward (co-producer) Alison Owen Mary Richards (line)
Endless Love	1981	Franco Zeffirelli	Judith Rascoe Scott Spencer (novel)	Keith Barish (executive) Dyson Lovell
Fargo	1996	Joel Coen	Joel Coen (written by) Ethan Coen (written by)	Tim Bevan (executive) John Cameron (line) Ethan Coen Eric Fellner (executive)
Fear, Anxiety & Depression	1989	Todd Solondz	Todd Solondz	Steve Golin Michael Kuhn Sigurjon Sighvatsson Nigel Sinclair Stan Wlodkowski
Fools of Fortune	1990	Pat O'Connor	Michael Hirst William Trevor (novel)	Tim Bevan (executive) Graham Bradstreet (executive) Caroline Hewitt (associate) Sarah Radclyffe
Force majeure	1989	Pierre Jolivet	Pierre Jolivet Olivier Schatzky	
Foreign Student	1994	Eva Sereny	Philippe Labro (novel The Foreign Student) Menno Meyjes	Mark Lombardo Silvio Muraglia (executive)
Four Weddings and a Funeral	1994	Mike Newell	Richard Curtis (written by)	Tim Bevan (executive) Richard Curtis (co-executive) Eric Fellner (executive) Duncan Kenworthy
Foxes	1980	Adrian Lyne	Gerald Ayres	Gerald Ayres David Puttnam
French Kiss	1995	Lawrence Kasdan	Adam Brooks (written by)	Tim Bevan Liza Chasin (associate) Eric Fellner Kathryn F. Galan Charles Okun (executive) Meg Ryan
Game, The	1997	David Fincher	John D. Brancato (written by) Michael Ferris (written by)	John D. Brancato (co-producer) CeÆn Chaffin Michael Ferris (co-producer) Steve Golin Jonathan Mostow (executive)
Garcu, Le	1995	Maurice Pialat	Sylvie Danton Maurice Pialat	Philippe Godeau

Cinematograhy	Film Editing	Special Effects	Production Design	Costume Design	Cast includes
Remi Adefarasin	Jill Bilcock	George Gibbs Clive R. Kay	John Myhre	Alexandra Byrne	
David Watkin	Michael J. Sheridan	Connie Brink	Ed Wittstein	Kristi Zea	Brooke Shields Martin Hewitt Shirley Knight Don Murray
Roger Deakins	Ethan Coen (as Roderick Jaynes) Joel Coen (as Roderick Jaynes)	Bruce R. Anderson Joe Carroll Michael Kranz Paul Murphy Ole Dieter Sturm Yvonne Sturm	Rick Heinrichs	Mary Zophres	William H. Macy Steve Buscemi Peter Stormare Frances McDormand
Stefan Czapsky	Peter Austin Emily Paine Barry Rubinow		Marek Dobrowolski	Susan Lyall	
Jerzy Zielinski	Michael Bradsell	Brian Warner	Jamie Leonard	Judy Moorcroft	Iain Glen Mary Elizabeth Mastrantonio Sean T. McClory Frankie McCafferty
Bertrand Chatry	Jean-Franois Naudon		Eric Simon		Patrick Bruel Franois Cluzet Kristin Scott Thomas Alan Bates
Franco Di Giacomo	Peter Hollywood		Howard Cummings		Robin Givens Marco Hofschneider Rick Johnson Charlotte Ross
Michael Coulter	Jon Gregory	Ian Wingrove	Maggie Gray	Lindy Hemming	Hugh Grant James Fleet Simon Callow John Hannah
Leon Bijou Paul Ryan	James Coblentz				Jodie Foster Cherie Currie Marilyn Kagan Kandice Stroh
Owen Roizman	Joe Hutshing	Gibert Pierri	Jon Hutman	Joanna Johnston	Meg Ryan Kevin Kline Timothy Hutton Jean Reno
Harris Savides	Jim Haygood	Eric Roberts Shawn Roberts Cliff Wenger	Jeffrey Beecroft	Michael Kaplan	Michael Douglas Sean Penn Deborah Unger James Rebhorn
	Herv de Luze		Olivier Radot	Martine Rapin	Grard Depardieu Graldine Pailhas Antoine Pialat Dominique Rocheteau

Title	Year	Director	Writing Credits	Produced by
Gingerbread Man, The	1998	Robert Altman	John Grisham Robert Altman (as Al Hayes)	Todd R. Baker (executive) Mark Burg (executive) David Levy (associate) Jeremy Tannenbaum Glen Tobias (executive)
Giorgino	1994	Laurent Boutonnat	Laurent Boutonnat Gilles Laurent	Laurent Boutonnat
Gnome Named Gnorm, A	1992	Stan Winston	Pen Densham (story) Pen Densham (screenplay) John Watson (screenplay)	Robert W. Cort Pen Densham Lawrence Kasanoff (executive) Scott Kroopf Richard Barton Lewis Dennis Murphy (associate) Ellen Steloff (executive) John Watson (supervising)
Green Mile, The	1999	Frank Darabont	Stephen King (novel) Frank Darabont (screenplay)	Frank Darabont David Valdes
Gridlock'd	1997	Vondie Curtis-Hall	Vondie Curtis-Hall	Michael Bennett (co-producer) Ted Field (executive) Preston L. Holmes (co-executive) Erica Huggins Damian Jones Scott Kroopf (executive) Stan Lathan (co-executive) Steven Siebert (co-producer) Russell Simmons (executive) Paul Webster
Gun in Betty Lou's Handbag, The	1992	Allan Moyle	Grace Cary Bickley (written by)	Sarah Bowman (associate) Robert W. Cort (executive) Ted Field (executive) Ira Halberstadt (co-producer) Scott Kroopf Cynthia Sherman (co-producer)
Guy	1996	Michael Lindsay-Hogg	Kirby Dick	Vincent D'Onofrio Warren Robert Jason Rene Missel
Haine, La	1995	Mathieu Kassovitz	Mathieu Kassovitz	Adeline Lecallier (associate) Alain Rocca (associate) Christophe Rossignon Gilles Sacuto (line)
Halcyon Days	1995	Patrick Dewolf	Kerry Crabbe Patrick Dewolf	Philippe Carcassonne (associate) Philippe Guez Simon Perry
Hard Rain	1998	Mikael Salomon	Graham Yost (written by)	Ian Bryce Mark Gordon Gary Levinsohn Art Levinson Allison Lyon Segan (executive) Christian Slater (co-producer)

Cinematograhy	Film Editing	Special Effects	Production Design	Costume Design	Cast includes
Changwei Gu	Geraldine Peroni	Ken Gorrell Thomas Kittle Casey Peterson David Tyrrell Russell Tyrrell	Stephen Altman	Dona Granata	Kenneth Branagh Embeth Davidtz Robert Downey Jr Daryl Hannah
Jean-Pierre Sauvaire	Laurent Boutonnat Agns Mouchel		Pierre Guffroy	Carine Sarfati	John Abineri Joss Ackland Jean-Pierre Aumont Frances Barber
Bojan Bazelli	Marcus Manton	Patrick L. Dalton Joe Knott Joe Montenegro Randy Willard Robert G. Willard Jerry D. Williams	Marcia Hinds	Audrey M. Bansmer	Anthony Michael Hall Jerry Orbach Claudia Christian Eli Danker
David Tattersall	Richard Francis-Bruce	Jason Gustafson	Terence Marsh	Karyn Wagner	Tom Hanks David Morse Bonnie Hunt Michael Clarke Duncan
Bill Pope	Christopher Koefoed	Tom Bender Greg W. Davidson Greg Landerer	Dan Bishop	Marie France	Tupac Shakur Tim Roth Vondie Curtis-Hall Thandie Newton
Charles Minsky	Janice Hampton Erica Huggins	Connie Brink Larry Fioritto	Michael Corenblith	Lisa Jensen	Penelope Ann Miller Eric Thal Alfre Woodard Julianne Moore
Arturo Smith	Dody Dorn		Kara Lindstrom		
Pierre Am	Mathieu Kassovitz Scott Stevenson		Giuseppe Ponturo	Virginie Montel	Vincent Cassel Hubert Koundé Sad Taghmaoui Abdel Ahmed Ghili
Patrick Blossier	Joºlle Hache Chris Wimble		Bernd Lepel	Tom Rand	Stephen Dorff Gabrielle Anwar Adrian Dunbar Sophie Aubry
Peter Menzies Jr.	Paul Hirsch	David Amborn Taylor Ball John Frazier Brandon Ramos Steve Riley James D. Schwalm Dennis Skotak	J. Michael Riva	Kathleen Detoro	Morgan Freeman Christian Slater Randy Quaid Minnie Driver

Title	Year	Director	Writing Credits	Produced by
Hi-Lo Country, The	1998	Stephen Frears	Max Evans (novel) Walon Green (screenplay)	Tim Bevan Liza Chasin (co-producer) Barbara De Fina Eric Fellner Martin Scorsese Rudd Simmons (executive)
Holy Matrimony	1994	Leonard Nimoy	David Weisberg (written by) Douglas S. Cook (written by)	Lane Janger Diana Phillips (co-producer) William Stuart
Home for the Holidays	1995	Jodie Foster	Chris Radant (short story) W.D. Richter (screenplay)	Jodie Foster Stuart Kleinman (executive) Peggy Rajski
Home of Our Own, A	1993	Tony Bill	Patrick Sheane Duncan (written by)	Bill Borden Dale Polloc
House of Cards	1993	Michael Lessac	Michael Lessac (story) Robert Jay Litz (story) Michael Lessac (screenplay)	Vittorio Cecchi Gori (executive) Wolfgang Glattes Lianne Halfon Gianni Nunnari (co-executive) Dale Pollock Jonathan Sanger (co-producer)
How to Be a Player	1997	Lionel C. Martin	Mark Brown (story) Mark Brown (screenplay) Demetria Johnson (screenplay)	Todd R. Baker Mark Burg Preston L. Holmes Stan Lathan (executive) Joanna Milter (co-producer) Carrie Morrow (co-producer) Robert F. Newmyer (executive) Rose Catherine Pinkney (co-producer) Jeffrey Silver (executive) Russell Simmons
Hudsucker Proxy, The	1994	Joel Coen	Ethan Coen (written by) Joel Coen (written by) Sam Raimi (written by)	Tim Bevan (executive) Ethan Coen Eric Fellner (executive) Graham Place (co-producer)
Huitime jour, Le	1996	Jaco van Dormael	Jaco van Dormael	Philippe Godeau Dominique Josset (executive) Eric Rommeluere (executive)
Indecent Woman aka Onfatsoenlijke vrouw, De	1991	Ben Verbong	Marianne Dikker Peter Mrthesheimer Jean van de Velde	Haig Balian Chris Brouwer Arnold Heslenfeld (line)
Jack and Sarah	1995	Tim Sullivan	Tim Sullivan	Simon Channing-Williams Pippa Cross Janette Day Alexandre Heylen (co-producer) Steve Morrison (executive)
Jason's Lyric	1994	Doug McHenry	Bobby Smith Jr. (written by)	Clarence Avant (executive) Suzanne Broderick (executive) Bill Carraro (associate) George Jackson Doug McHenry Marilla Ross (co-executive) Bobby Smith Jr. (co-producer) Dwight Williams (co-producer)

Cinematograhy	Film Editing	Special Effects	Production Design	Costume Design	Cast includes
Oliver Stapleton	Masahiro Hirakubo	Ole Dieter Sturm	Patricia Norris	Patricia Norris	Woody Harrelson Billy Crudup Patricia Arquette Cole Hauser
Bobby Bukowski	Peter E. Berger		Edward Pisoni	Deena Appel	Patricia Arquette Joseph Gordon-Levitt Armin Mueller-Stahl Tate Donovan
Lajos Koltai	Lynzee Klingman	Kathleen Tonkin Robert Vazquez	Andrew McAlpine	Susan Lyall	Holly Hunter Robert Downey Jr Anne Bancroft Charles Durning
Jean Lpine					Kathy Bates Edward Furlong Clarissa Lassig Sarah Schaub
Victor Hammer	Walter Murch	Greg Hull	Peter S. Larkin	Marina Marit (key costumer) Julie Weiss	Kathleen Turner Tommy Lee Jones Asha Menina Shiloh Strong
	William Young		Bruce Curtis	Mimi Melgaard	Bill Bellamy Natalie Desselle Lark Voorhies Mari Morrow
Roger Deakins	Thom Noble	Roderic 'Mick' Duff Ralph Kerr	Dennis Gassner	Richard Hornung	Tim Robbins Jennifer Jason Leigh Paul Newman Charles Durning
Walther van den Ende	Susana Rossberg			Yan Tax	Daniel Auteuil Pascal Duquenne Miou-Miou Henri Garcin
Lex Wertwijn	Ton de Graaff		Dick Schillemans	Tamara Jongsma	Jos Way Coen van Vrijberghe de Coningh Huub Stape Lydia van Nergena
Jean-Yves Escoffier	Lesley Walker		Christopher J. Bradshaw	Dany Everett	Richard E. Grant Samantha Mathis Judi Dench Eileen Atkins
Francis Kenny	Andrew Mondshein	Bob Williams	Simon Dobbin	Craig Anthony	Allen Payne Jada Pinkett Bokeem Woodbine Anthony 'Treach' Criss

Title	Year	Director	Writing Credits	Produced by
Johnsons, De	1992	Rudolf van den Berg	Roy Frumkes (story) Rocco Simonelli Leon de Winter	Haig Balian Chris Brouwer Arnold Heslenfeld (executive)
Jude	1996	Michael Winterbotto	Hossein Amini Thomas Hardy (novel Jude the Obscure)	Andrew Eaton Sheila Fraser Milne (associate) Mark Shivas (executive) Stewart Till (executive)
Just Your Luck aka Whiskey Down	1996	Gary Auerbach	Todd Alcott Gary Auerbach (also story)	Stan Bernstein Gregory Cundiff Stephen Gelber (executive) William S. Gilmore (associate) Melanie Luciano Brian Lutz W. Mark McNair (line)
Kalifornia	1993	Dominic Sena	Stephen Levy (story) Tim Metcalfe (story) Tim Metcalfe (screenplay)	Lynn Bigelow (executive producer) Steve Golin (producer) Gregory Goodman (line producer) Jim Kouf (executive producer) Aristides McGarry (producer) Mitch Sacharoff (co-producer) Kristine J. Schwarz (co-producer) Sigurjon Sighvatsson (producer)
Kazaam	1996	Paul Michael Glaser	Paul Michael Glaser (story) Christian Ford (screenplay) Roger Soffer (screenplay)	Leonard Armato (executive) Bruce Binkow (co-executive) Robert W. Cort (executive) Robert Engelman Ted Field (executive) Paul Michael Glaser (as Paul M. Glaser) Michael A. Helfant (co-executive) Beth Maloney Jelin (co-executive) Scott Kroopf Shaquille O'Neal (executive)
Keys to Tulsa	1997	Leslie Greif	Brian Fair Berkey (novel) Harley Peyton (screenplay)	Michael Birnbaum (executive) David Gaines (associate) Kenny Golde (associate) Leslie Greif Peter Isacksen (executive) Andrew G. La Marca (line) Guy J. Louthan (co-producer) Harley Peyton Elliot Lewis Rosenblatt (line)
Kill Me Again	1989	John Dahl	John Dahl David W. Warfield	Scott Cameron (associate) Steve Golin Michael Kuhn (executive) Carol Lewis (associate) George J. Roewe III (line) Sigurjon Sighvatsson Nigel Sinclair (executive) David W. Warfield
King of the Hill	1993	Steven Soderbergh	A.E. Hotchner (book) Steven Soderbergh (screenplay)	Albert Berger John Hardy (executive) Barbara Maltby Ron Yerxa
King of the Mountain	1981	Noel Nosseck	David Barry (article) H.R. Christian	Jeffrey Benjamin (associate) Jack Frost Sanders William Tennant (executive)

Cinematograhy	Film Editing	Special Effects	Production Design	Costume Design	Cast includes
Theo Bierkens	Wim Louwrier	Sjoerd Didden Ken Lailey Floris Schuller	Harry Ammerlaan	Jany Temime	Esme de la Bretonire Kenneth Herdigein Monique van de Ven Gerda Havertong
Eduardo Serra	Trevor Waite	John Markwell	Joseph Bennett	Janty Yates	Christopher Eccleston Kate Winslet Liam Cunningham Rachel Griffiths
Roberto Schaefer	Larry Bock	William D. Harrison Nick Plantico	Chuck Conner	Nina Canter	Sean Patrick Flanery Virginia Madsen Carroll Baker Bill Erwin
Bojan Bazelli	Martin Hunter	James Burkart David Fletcher Jeffrey Knott Michael Schorr	Michael White	Kelle Kutsugeras	Brad Pitt Juliette Lewis David Duchovny Michelle Forbes
Charles Minsky	Michael E. Polakow	Tom Chesney Chris Perry Frederic Soumagnas	Donald Graham Burt	Hope Hanafin	Shaquille O'Neal Francis Capra Ally Walker James Acheson
Robert Fraisse	Eric L. Beason Louis F. Cioffi Michael R. Miller		Derek R. Hill	Marie France	Eric Stoltz Cameron Diaz Randy Graff Dennis Letts
Jacques Steyn	Eric L. Beason Frank E. Jimenez Jonathan P. Shaw	Carol McCarthy Robert E. McCarthy	Michelle Minch	Terry Dresbach	Pat Mulligan Nick Dimitri Michael Madsen Joanne Whalley
Elliot Davis	Steven Soderbergh	J.D. Streett	Gary Frutkoff	Susan Lyall	Jesse Bradford Jeroen Krabbé Lisa Eichhorn Karen Allen
Donald Peterman	William Steinkamp	Roy L. Downey	James H. Spencer	Susan Becker	Harry Hamlin Joseph Bottoms Deborah Van Valkenburgh Richard Cox

Title	Year	Director	Writing Credits	Produced by
Land Girls, The	1998	David Leland	Angela Huth (novel) Keith Dewhurst David Leland	Ruth Jackson (executive) Simon Relph Andrew Warren (co-producer)
Life Less Ordinary, A	1997	Danny Boyle	John Hodge	Sophie Byrne (animation) Margaret Hilliard (line) Andrew Macdonald
Little Death, The	1995	Jan Verheyen	Nicholas Bogner (written by) Michael Holden (written by)	Mark Burg (executive) Ann Dubinet Dan Genetti (executive) Carrie Morrow (co-producer) Chris Zarpas
Loch Ness	1995	John Henderson	John Fusco	Nicky Kentish Barnes (co-producer) Tim Bevan Eric Fellner (executive) Debra Hayward (associate) Judith Hunt (co-producer) Stephen Ujlaki
Lock, Stock and Two Smoking Barrels	1998	Guy Ritchie	Guy Ritchie	Stephen Marks (executive) Georgia Masters (co-producer) Peter Morton (executive) Angad Paul (executive) Sebastian Pearson (associate) Jan Roldanus (associate) Trudie Styler (executive) Steve Tisch (executive) Ronaldo Vasconcellos (line) Matthew Vaughn
London Kills Me	1991	Hanif Kureishi	Hanif Kureishi	Tim Bevan Graham Bradstreet
Man and Two Women, A aka Un homme et deux femmes	1991	Valrie Stroh	Ren Fret Doris Lessing (shorts Un homme et deux femmes; L'Un, l'autre; Notre amie Judith) Valrie Stroh	Ren Fret
Mandela	1996	Angus Gibson Jo Menell	Bo Widerberg	Chris Blackwell (executive) Jonathan Demme Amina Frense (associate) Jo Menell Peter Saraf (co-producer) Edward Saxon Richard Stengel (associate)

Cinematograhy	Film Editing	Special Effects	Production Design	Costume Design	Cast includes
Henry Braham	Nicholas Moore	Jeff Clifford Steve Petts Ian Wingrove	Caroline Amies	Shuna Harwood	Catherine McCormack Rachel Weisz Anna Friel Steven Mackintosh
Brian Tufano	Masahiro Hirakubo	Paul Kelly B.J. Shelley Bob Shelley	Kave Quinn	Rachael Fleming	Holly Hunter Delroy Lindo Dan Hedaya Cameron Diaz Ewan McGregor
David Phillips	Joseph Gutowski	Mark DiSarro	Armin Ganz	Mimi Melgaard	Brent Fraser Solomon Burke Johnny Williams Pamela Gidley
Clive Tickner	Jon Gregory	J.D. Streett	Sophie Becher	Nic Ede	Ted Danson Joely Richardson Ian Holm Harris Yulin
Tim Maurice-Jones	Niven Howie		Iain Andrews Eve Mavrakis	Stephanie Collie	Jason Flemyng Dexter Fletcher Nick Moran Jason Statham
Edward Lachman	Jon Gregory		Stuart Walker	Amy Roberts	Justin Chadwick Fiona Shaw Brad Dourif Naveen Andrews
Peter Suschitzky	Charlotte Fauvel		Georges Stoll	Barbara Kidd	Valrie Stroh Lambert Wilson Diane Pierens Olivia Brunaux
Dewald Aukema Peter Tischhauser	Andy Keir			Renette Bengtsson ¯sa Broms Lotta Petersson Birthe Qualmann Nicklas stergren	Nelson Mandela Winnie Mandela

Title	Year	Director	Writing Credits	Produced by
Map of the Human Heart	1992	Vincent Ward	Louis Nowra Vincent Ward (story)	Linda Beath (co-producer) Tim Bevan Graham Bradstreet (executive) Redmond Morris (associate) Sylvaine Sainderichin (co-producer) Paul Saltzman (co-producer) Vincent Ward Bob Weinstein (executive) Harvey Weinstein (executive) Timothy White (co-producer)
MatchMaker, The	1997	Mark Joffe	Greg Dinner (earlier screenplay) Karen Janszen (screenplay) Louis Nowra (screenplay) Graham Linehan (screenplay)	Nicky Kentish Barnes (line) Tim Bevan Liza Chasin (co-producer) Eric Fellner Lyn Goleby (executive) Debra Hayward (co-producer) Katy McGuinness (Irish co-producer for the Good Film Co.) Luc Roeg
Midnight Clear, A	1991	Keith Gordon	William Wharton (novel) Keith Gordon (screenplay)	Marc Abraham (executive) Armyan Bernstein (executive) Bill Borden Margaret Hilliard (associate) Dale Pollock Tom Rosenberg (executive)
Midnight Express	1978	Alan Parker	Billy Hayes (book) William Hoffer (book) Oliver Stone	Peter Guber (executive) Alan Marshall (IV) David Puttnam
Monsieur Hire	1989	Patrice Leconte	Georges Simenon (novel Les Fianailles de M. Hire) Patrice Leconte Patrick Dewolf	Philippe Carcassonne Ren Cleitman
Moonlight and Valentino	1995	David Anspaugh	Ellen Simon (play) Ellen Simon (screenplay)	Tim Bevan Liza Chasin (associate) Eric Fellner Mary McLaglen (co-producer) Alison Owen
Mr. Holland's Opus	1995	Stephen Herek	Patrick Sheane Duncan (written by)	Robert W. Cort Patrick Sheane Duncan (executive) Ted Field Judith James (co-producer) Scott Kroopf (executive) Michael Nolin William Teitler (co-producer)
Mr. Reliable	1996	Nadia Tass	Don Catchlove Terry Hayes	Michael Hamlyn Terry Hayes Dennis Kiely (line) Jim McElroy
Mulholland Falls	1996	Lee Tamahori	Peter Dexter (story) Floyd Mutrux (story) Peter Dexter (screenplay)	Mario Iscovich (executive) Lili Fini Zanuck Richard D. Zanuck
Nell	1994	Michael Apted	Mark Handley (play Idioglossia) William Nicholson (screenplay) Mark Handley (screenplay)	Jodie Foster Rene Missel Graham Place (co-producer)

Cinematograhy	Film Editing	Special Effects	Production Design	Costume Design	Cast includes
Eduardo Serra	John Scott Frans Vandenburg	Richard Conway	John Beard	Rene April Penny Rose	Jason Scott Lee Anne Parillaud Patrick Bergin John Cusack
Ellery Ryan	Paul Martin Smith	Graham Bushe Mick Doyle Maurice Foley	Mark Geraghty	Howard Burden	Janeane Garofalo David O'Hara Milo O'Shea Jay O. Sanders
Tom Richmond	Don Brochu	Rick Josephsen Ken Nosack	David Nichols	Barbara Tfank	Peter Berg Kevin Dillon Arye Gross Ethan Hawke
Michael Seresin	Gerry Hambling		Geoffrey Kirkland	Milena Canonero	Brad Davis Irene Miracle Bo Hopkins Paolo Bonacelli
Denis Lenoir	Joºlle Hache		Yvan Maussion	Elisabeth Tavernier	Michel Blanc Sandrine Bonnaire Luc Thuillier Andr Wilms
Julio Macat	David Rosenbloom	Michael Kavanagh Tony Kenny	Robb Wilson King	Denise Cronenberg	Elizabeth Perkins Whoopi Goldberg Shadia Simmons Erica Luttrell
Oliver Wood	Trudy Ship	Bob Riggs	David Nichols	Aggie Guerard Rodgers	Richard Dreyfuss Glenne Headly Jay Thomas Olympia Dukakis
David Parker	Peter Carrodus		Jon Dowding	Tess Schofield	Colin Friels Gillian Statham Gillian Graham Rebecca Di Corpo
Haskell Wexler	Sally Menke	Samuel E. Price Thomas R. Ward	Richard Sylbert	Ellen Mirojnick	Nick Nolte Melanie Griffith Chazz Palminteri Michael Madsen
Dante Spinotti	Jim Clark	Robert Vazquez	Jon Hutman	Susan Lyall	Jodie Foster Liam Neeson Natasha Richardson Richard Libertini

Title	Year	Director	Writing Credits	Produced by
New Jersey Drive	1995	Nick Gomez	Nick Gomez (also story) Michel Marriott (story)	Bob Gosse Spike Lee (executive) Larry Meistrich Rudd Simmons (co-producer)
No Looking Back	1998	Edward Burns	Edward Burns	Alysse Bezahler (line) Edward Burns Ted Hope Michael Nozik Robert Redford (executive) John Sloss (co-executive)
Notting Hill	1999	Roger Michell	Richard Curtis	Tim Bevan (executive) Richard Curtis (executive) Eric Fellner (executive) Duncan Kenworthy Mary Richards (line)
Nuits fauves, Les aka Savage Nights	1992	Cyril Collard	Cyril Collard Jacques Fieschi (adaptation)	Nella Banfi Jean-Frdric Samie (executive)
Nurse Betty	2000	Neil LaBute	John C. Richards (story) John C. Richards (screenplay) James Flamberg (screenplay)	Moritz Borman (executive) Steve Golin W. Mark McNair (associate) Gail Mutrux Stephen Pevner (executive) Albert M. Shapiro (associate) Chris Sievernich (executive) Philip Steuer (executive)
Operation Dumbo Drop	1995	Simon Wincer	James Morris (IV) (story) Gene Quintano (written by) Jim Kouf (written by)	Robert W. Cort (executive) Ted Field (executive) Penelope L. Foster (co-producer) Edward Gold (co-executive) Diane Nabatoff
Panther	1995	Mario Van Peebles	Melvin Van Peebles (novel Panther) Melvin Van Peebles (screenplay)	Tim Bevan (executive) Lisa Chassin (associate) Robert De Niro (uncredited) Eric Fellner (executive) Preston L. Holmes Mario Van Peebles Melvin Van Peebles
Paperback Hero	1998	Antony J. Bowman	Antony J. Bowman (novel)	Lance W. Reynolds Dani Rogers (co-producer) John Winter
Paws	1997	Karl Zwicky	Harry Cripps (also story) Karl Zwicky (story)	Andrena Finlay Brenda Pam (associate) Rebel Russell (executive) Vicki Watson
Photographing Fairies	1997	Nick Willing	Chris Harrald Steve Szilagyi (book) Nick Willing	Michelle Camarda Alan Greenspan (executive) Mike Newell (executive) Fonda Snyder (co-producer) Lawrence Weinberg (co-producer)
Pig's Tale, A aka Summer Camp	1995	Paul Tassie	Todd Richardson (story) Todd Richardson (screenplay) Scott Sandorf (screenplay) Charles Ransom (screenplay)	Tim Clawson (supervising) Steve Golin (executive) Gregory Goodman Matthew Loze Sigurjon Sighvatsson (executive) Lynn Weimer (co-producer)

Cinematograhy	Film Editing	Special Effects	Production Design	Costume Design	Cast includes
Adam Kimmel	Jane Pia Abramowitz (associate) Tracy Granger		Lester Cohen	Ellen Lutter	Christine Baranski Samantha Brown Gabriel Casseus Sharron Corley
Frank Prinzi	Susan Graef		Thrse DePrez	Sarah Jane Slotnick	Lauren Holly Edward Burns Jon Bon Jovi Connie Britton
Michael Coulter	Nicholas Moore	Timothy Webber	Stuart Craig	Shuna Harwood	Julia Roberts Hugh Grant Richard McCabe Rhys Ifans
Manuel TerÆn	Lise Beaulieu		Jacky Macchi	Rgine Arniaud	Cyril Collard Romane Bohringer Carlos Lpez Corinne Blue
Jean-Yves Escoffie	Joel Plotch Steven Weisberg	Liz Anderson Rick Bongiovanni	Charles Breen	Lynette Meyer	Morgan Freeman Rene Zellweger Chris Rock Greg Kinnear
Russell Boyd	O. Nicholas Brown	Brian Cox	Paul Peters	Rosanna Norton	Danny Glover Ray Liotta Denis Leary Doug E. Doug
Edward J. Pei	Earl Watson	Beverley Hartigan	Richard Hoover	Paul Simmons	Kadeem Hardison Bokeem Woodbine Joe Don Baker Courtney B. Vance
David Burr	Veronika Jenet		Jon Dowding	Louise Wakefield	Claudia Karvan Hugh Jackman Angie Milliken Andrew S. Gilbert
Geoff Burton	Nicholas Holmes		Steven Jones-Evans	David Rowe	Billy Connolly Nathan Cavaleri Emilie Franois Sandy Gore
John de Borman	Sean Barton	Rachael Penfold	Laurence Dorman	Hazel Pethig	Emily Woof Frances Barber Philip Davis Toby Stephens
Ronald Vctor Garca	Lou Angelo	Lou Carlucci Chuck Schmitz	Nicholas T. Preovolos	Terry Dresbach	Joe Flaherty Sean Babb Mike Damus Jonathan Hilario

Title	Year	Director	Writing Credits	Produced by
Plunkett & Macleane	1999	Jake Scott	Selwyn Roberts (earlier screenplay) Robert Wade (screenplay) Neal Purvis (screenplay) Charles McKeown (screenplay)	Tim Bevan Eric Fellner Jonathan Finn (co-producer) Rupert Harvey Gary Oldman (executive) Selwyn Roberts (executive) Matthew Stillman (executive) Douglas Urbanski (executive) Natascha Wharton (co-producer)
Portrait of a Lady, The	1996	Jane Campion	Henry James (novel) Laura Jones	Steve Golin (associate) Monty Montgomery Mark Turnbull Ann Wingate (co-producer)
Posse	1993	Mario Van Peebles	Sy Richardson Dario Scardapane	Tim Bevan (executive) James Bigwood (associate) Eric Fellner (executive) Bill Fishman (co-executive) Jim Fishman (co-producer) Preston L. Holmes Jim Steele Paul Webster (co-executive)
Pred dozhdot aka Before the Rain	1994	Milcho Manchevski	Milcho Manchevski	Marc Baschet (co-producer) Judy Counihan Frdrique Dumas-Zajdela (co-producer) Cdomir Kolar Sheila Fraser Milne (associate) David Redman (associate) Paul Sarony (line) Sam Taylor Chris Thompson (line) Gordon Tozija (co-producer) Cat Villiers
Priest	1994	Antonia Bird	Jimmy McGovern	George Faber Joanna Newbery (associate) Mark Shivas (executive) Josephine Ward
Proposition, The	1998	Lesli Linka Glatter	Rick Ramage (written by)	Ted Field Scott Kroopf Diane Nabatoff Lata Ryan (executive) Alessandro F. Uzielli (co-executive)
Pursuit of D.B. Cooper, The	1981	Roger Spottiswoode	J.D. Reed (book Free Fall) Jeffrey Alan Fiskin	Don Kranze (executive) (as Donald Kranze) Ron Shelton (associate) Michael Taylor William Tennant (executive) Dan Wigutow
P.I. Private Investigations	1987	Nigel Dick		
Red Rock West	1992	John Dahl	John Dahl (written by) Rick Dahl (written by)	Rick Dahl (associate) Steve Golin Michael Kuhn (executive) Jane McGann (executive) Sigurjon Sighvatsson Lynn Weimer (associate)

Cinematograhy	Film Editing	Special Effects	Production Design	Costume Design	Cast includes
John Mathieson	Oral Norrie Ottley		Norris Spencer	Janty Yates	Jonny Lee Miller Iain Robertson Robert Carlyle Ken Stott
Stuart Dryburgh	Veronika Jenet		Janet Patterson	Janet Patterson	Nicole Kidman John Malkovich Barbara Hershey Mary-Louise Parker
Peter Menzies Jr.	Mark Conte	Thomas C. Ford	Catherine Hardwicke	Paul Simmons	Mario Van Peebles Stephen Baldwin Charles Lane Tom 'Tiny' Lister Jr
Darius Khondji Manuel TerÆn	Nicolas Gaster	John Fontana Valentin Lozev	Sharon Lomofsky David Munns	Caroline Harris Sue Yelland	Katrin Cartlidge Rade Serbedzija Grgoire Colin Labina Mitevska
Fred Tammes	Susan Spivey		Raymond Langhorn	Jill Taylor	Linus Roache Tom Wilkinson Robert Carlyle Cathy Tyson
Peter Sova	Jacqueline Cambas	William 'Billy Jack' Jakielaszek Brian Ricci Ed Ricci Stephen R. Ricci	David Brisbin	Anna B. Sheppard	Robert Loggia Bronia Wheeler Kenneth Branagh Madeleine Stowe
Harry Stradling Jr. Charles F. Wheeler	Allan Jaco Robbe Roberts	Bill Bailes Gene Grigg	E. Preston Ames		Robert Duvall Treat Williams Kathryn Harrold Ed Flanders
			Piers Plowden		Martin Balsam Talia Balsam Big Yank Desiree Boschetti
Marc Reshovsky	Scott Chestnut	John Carl Buechler Mark R. Byers Frank Ceglia John Foster Dean Gates Ted Haynes Rod Matsui	Robert Pearson	Terry Dresbach	Nicolas Cage Craig Reay Vance Johnson Robert Apel

Title	Year	Director	Writing Credits	Produced by
Relic, The	1997	Peter Hyams	Douglas Preston (novel) Lincoln Child (novel) Amy Holden Jones (screenplay) John Raffo (screenplay) Rick Jaffa (screenplay) Amanda Silver (screenplay)	Mark Gordon (executive) Gale Anne Hurd Gary Levinsohn (executive) Sam Mercer
Return to Paradise	1998	Joseph Ruben	Pierre Jolivet (motion picture Force Majeure) O. Schatzky (motion picture Force Majeure) Wesley Strick (screenplay) Bruce Robinson (screenplay)	David Arnold (executive) Alain Bernheim Steve Golin Ezra Swerdlow (executive)
Ridicule	1996	Patrice Leconte	Rmi Waterhouse Michel Fessler Eric Vicaut	Frdric Brillion Philippe Carcassonne Gilles Legrand
Robin Hood	1991	John Irvin	Sam Resnick (story) Sam Resnick (teleplay) John McGrath (teleplay)	Tim Bevan Sarah Radclyffe
Romeo Is Bleeding	1993	Peter Medak	Hilary Henkin (written by)	Tim Bevan (executive) Eric Fellner (executive) Michael Flynn (co-producer) Hilary Henkin Paul Webster
Roommates	1995	Peter Yates	Max Apple (short story) Max Apple (story) Max Apple (screenplay) Stephen Metcalfe (screenplay)	Max Apple (associate) Robert W. Cort Ted Field Ira Halberstadt (executive) Scott Kroopf Adam Leipzig (executive)
Rubin and Ed	1991	Trent Harris	Trent Harris (written by)	Damian Jones (associate) Paul Webster
Ruby	1992	John Mackenzie	Stephen Davis (play Love Field) Stephen Davis (screenplay)	Steve Golin Michael Kuhn (executive) Jay Roewe (co-producer) Sigurjon Sighvatsson Lynn Weimer (associate) Richard S. Wright (associate)
Shallow Grave	1994	Danny Boyle	John Hodge	Andrew Macdonald Allan Scott (executive)
Six Weeks	1982	Tony Bill	David Seltzer	Peter Guber Jon Peters Hillary Anne Ripps (associate)
Sleepers	1996	Barry Levinson	Lorenzo Carcaterra (book) Barry Levinson (screenplay)	Lorenzo Carcaterra (co-producer) Peter Giuliano (executive) Steve Golin Barry Levinson Gerrit van der Meer (associate)
Snow White	1997	Michael Cohn	Jacob Ludwig Carl Grimm (story) Wilhelm Carl Grimm (story) Thomas E. Szollosi (screenplay) Deborah Serra (screenplay)	Robert W. Cort (executive) Tom Engelman Ted Field (executive) Scott Kroopf (executive) Tim Van Rellim (co-producer)

Cinematograhy	Film Editing	Special Effects	Production Design	Costume Design	Cast includes
Peter Hyams	Steven Kemper	Gary Elmendorf	Philip Harrison	Daniel J. Lester Stan Winston	Penelope Ann Miller Tom Sizemore Linda Hunt James Whitmore
Reynaldo Villalobos	Craig McKay Andrew Mondshein	Craig Barron	Bill Groom	Juliet Polcsa	Vince Vaughn Anne Heche Joaquin Phoenix David Conrad
Thierry Arbogast	Joºlle Hache		Yvan Maussion	Christian Gasc	Charles Berling Jean Rochefort Fanny Ardant Judith Godrche
Jason Lehel	Peter Tanner				Daniel Webb Conrad Asquith Barry Stanton Patrick Bergin
Dariusz Wolski	Walter Murch	Mark Berg Wilfred Caban Steven Kirshoff	Stuart Wurtzel	Aude Bronson-Howard	Gary Oldman Wallace Wood Juliette Lewis David Proval
Mike Southon	Seth Flaum John Tintori		Dan Bishop Douglas Higgins	Linda Donahue	Peter Falk D.B. Sweeney Julianne Moore Ellen Burstyn
Bryan Duggan	Brent A. Schoenfeld		Clark Hunter	Lawane Cole	Crispin Glover Howard Hesseman Karen Black Michael Greene
Phil Meheux	Richard Trevor	Ken Estes John M. Wells	David Brisbin	Susie DeSanto	Frank Orsatti Sherilyn Fenn Jeffrey Nordling Danny Aiello
Brian Tufano	Masahiro Hirakubo	Tony Steers	Kave Quinn	Kate Carin	Kerry Fox Christopher Eccleston Ewan McGregor Ken Stott
Michael D. Margulies	Stu Linder		Sandy Veneziano		Dudley Moore Mary Tyler Moore Katherine Healy Shannon Wilcox
Michael Ballhaus	Stu Linder	Mark Bero Wilfred Caban Steven Kirshoff Michael Wood	Kristi Zea	Gloria Gresham	Kevin Bacon Billy Crudup Robert De Niro Ron Eldard
Mike Southon	Ian Crafford	Ernest D. Farino Leslie Huntley Gene Warren Jr	Gemma Jackson	Marit Allen	Sigourney Weaver Sam Neill Gil Bellows Taryn Davis

Title	Year	Director	Writing Credits	Produced by
Spice World	1997	Bob Spiers	Kim Fuller Jamie Curtis (additional writing)	Uri Fruchtmann Kim Fuller (associate) Simon Fuller (executive) Peter McAleese (co-producer) Mark L. Rosen Barnaby Thompson
Split Image	1982	Ted Kotcheff	Robert Mark Kamen Robert Kaufman Scott Spence	Don Carmody (co-producer) Ted Kotcheff
Stranger Among Us, A	1992	Sidney Lumet	Robert J. Avrech (written by)	Robert J. Avrech (co-producer) Carol Baum (executive) Sandy Gallin (executive) Steve Golin Burtt Harris (line) Lilith Jacobs (associate) Howard Rosenman Sigurjon Sighvatsson Susan Tarr (co-producer)
S.F.W.	1994	Jefery Levy	Andrew Wellman (novel) Danny Rubin (screenplay) Jefery Levy (screenplay)	Gloria Lopez (associate) Michael Nelson (co-producer) Dale Pollock Sigurjon Sighvatsson (executive)
Tacones lejanos aka High Heels	1991	Pedro Almodvar	Pedro Almodvar (also story)	Agustn Almodvar (executive) Enrique Posner (associate)
Tango	1993	Patrice Leconte	Patrick Dewolf Patrice Leconte	Philippe Carcassonne (co-producer) Ren Cleitman (co-producer)
Temptation of a Monk aka You Seng	1993	Clara Law	Eddie Ling-Ching Fong Lillian Lee	Teddy Robin Kwan
Terminal Velocity	1994	Deran Sarafian	David N. Twohy (written by)	Joan Bradshaw (co-producer) Robert W. Cort (executive) Tom Engelman Ted Field (executive) Scott Kroopf David N. Twohy (executive)

Cinematograhy	Film Editing	Special Effects	Production Design	Costume Design	Cast includes
Clive Tickner	Andrea MacArthur	Paddy Eason Dan Glass Pete Hanson Rachael Penfold Tim Wellspring	Grenville Horner	Kate Carin	Melanie Brown Emma Bunton Melanie Chisholm Geri Halliwell Victoria Beckham
Robert C. Jessup	Jay Kamen		Wolf Kroeger		Michael O'Keefe Karen Allen Peter Fonda James Woods
Andrzej Bartkowiak	Andrew Mondshein	Gregory C. Tippie	Philip Rosenberg	Gary Jones Ann Roth	Melanie Griffith Eric Thal John Pankow Tracy Pollan
Peter Deming	Lauren Zuckerman	Frank Ceglia	Eve Cauley	Debra McGuire	Stephen Dorff Reese Witherspoon Jake Busey Joey Lauren Adams
Alfredo F. Mayo	Jos Salcedo	Reyes Abades	Pierre-Louis Thvenet	Giorgio Armani Coco Chanel Jos Mara De Cosso Peris	Victoria Abril Marisa Paredes Miguel Bosé Anna Lizaran
Eduardo Serra	Genevive Winding	Bernard Chevreul Jean-Pierre Suchet	Yvan Maussion	Ccile Magnan	Philippe Noiret Richard Bohringer Thierry Lhermitte Carole Bouquet
Andrew Lesnie	Jill Bilcock		Zhanjia Yang Timmy Yip		Joan Chen Michael Lee Lisa Lu Hsing-kuo Wu Fengyi Zhang
Oliver Wood	Peck Prior Frank J. Urioste	Lawrence J. Cavanaugh	David L. Snyder	Poppy Cannon-Reese	Charlie Sheen Nastassja Kinski James Gandolfini Christopher McDonald

Title	Year	Director	Writing Credits	Produced by
Thousand Acres, A	1997	Jocelyn Moorhouse	Jane Smiley (novel) Laura Jones (screenplay)	Marc Abraham Lynn Arost Armyan Bernstein (executive) Thomas A. Bliss (executive) Steve Golin Kate Guinzburg Michelle Pfeiffer Diana Pokorny (co-producer) Sigurjon Sighvatsson
Thursday	1998	Skip Woods	Skip Woods	W. Mark McNair (line) Alan Poul Christine Sheaks (co-producer) Skip Woods (co-producer)
Tie That Binds, The	1995	Wesley Strick	Michael Auerbach (written by)	Jon Brown (executive) Robert W. Cort (executive) Ted Field (executive) David Madden Patrick Markey John Morrissey Katherine Orrison (associate) Susan Zachary
Trainspotting	1996	Danny Boyle	Irvine Welsh (novel) John Hodge	Christopher Figg (co-producer) Andrew Macdonald
Two Much	1996	Fernando Trueba	Donald E. Westlake (novel) Fernando Trueba (screenplay) David Trueba (screenplay)	Robert W. Cort (executive) Paul Diamond (associate) Ted Field (executive) Fernando de Garcill.Æn (associate) Andrs Vicente Gmez Anglica Huete (line) Cristina Huete Adam Leipzig (executive) Volkert Struycken (associate) Fernando Trueba
Un coeur en hiver	1992	Claude Sautet	Jacques Fieschi Claude Sautet Jrme Tonnerre	Philippe Carcassonne Grard Gaultier (executive) Jean-Louis Livi
Unveiled	1994	William Cole	Jerome Cohen-Olivar (story) Michael Diamond Roger Kumble	Said Bencherki (co-producer) Daniele Cohen-Olivar (associate) Jerome Cohen-Olivar Albert Levy (co-producer) Zoubir Mahi Beatriz Sohni (line) Jacques Toledano (associate)
Usual Suspects, The	1995	Bryan Singer	Christopher McQuarrie (written by)	Hans Brockmann (executive) Franois Duplat (executive) Art Horan (executive) Robert Jones (executive) Kenneth Kokin (co-producer) Michael McDonnell Bryan Singer
U.F.O.	1994	Tony Dow	Roy 'Chubby' Brown Richard Hall Simon Wright	Paul Sarony (line) Peter Smith (executive) Simon Wright

Cinematograhy	Film Editing	Special Effects	Production Design	Costume Design	Cast includes
Tak Fujimoto	Marianne Brandon	Jennifer Law-Stump Jeff Wells	Dan Davis	Ruth Myers	Michelle Pfeiffer Jessica Lange Jennifer Jason Leigh Colin Firth
Denis Lenoir	Peter Schink Paul Trejo	Ryan Arndt Alex R. Felix John E. Gray Terry W. King	Chris Anthony Miller	Mark Bridges	Thomas Jane Aaron Eckhart Paulina Porizkova James LeGros
Bobby Bukowski	Michael N. Knue	Jeff Denes Richard Stutsman	Marcia Hinds	Betsy Heimann	Daryl Hannah Keith Carradine Moira Kelly Vincent Spano
Brian Tufano	Masahiro Hirakubo	Grant Mason Tony Steers	Kave Quinn	Rachael Fleming	Ewan McGregor Ewen Bremner Jonny Lee Miller Robert Carlyle
Jos Luis Alcaine	Nena Bernard	Richard Lee Jones	Juan Botella	Lala Huete	Antonio Banderas Melanie Griffith Daryl Hannah Danny Aiello
Yves Angelo	Jacqueline Thidot		Christian Marti	Corinne Jorry	Daniel Auteuil Emmanuelle Bart Andr Dussollier Elisabeth Bourgine
Ross Berryman	Adrian Carr	Daniel Cruder	Stuart Blatt	Linda L. Meltzer	Lisa Zane Nick Chinlund Whip Hubley Martha Gehman
Newton Thomas Sigel	John Ottman	Roy L. Downey Greg Hendrickson	Howard Cummings	Louise Mingenbach	Stephen Baldwin Gabriel Byrne Benicio Del Toro Kevin Pollak Kevin Spacey
Paul Wheeler	Geoff Hogg	Alan Whibley	David McHenry	Liz Da Costa	Roy 'Chubby' Brown Sara Stockbridge Amanda Symonds Roger Lloyd-Pack

Title	Year	Director	Writing Credits	Produced by
Very Bad Things	1998	Peter Berg	Peter Berg (written by)	Cindy Cowan Ted Field (executive) Laura Greenlee (line) Michael A. Helfant (executive) Scott Kroopf (executive) Diane Nabatoff Michael Schiffer Christian Slater (executive)
Waking the Dead	1999	Keith Gordon	Scott Spencer (novel) Robert Dillon (screenplay)	Jodie Foster (executive) Keith Gordon Stuart Kleinman Irene Litinsky (co-producer) Linda Reisman
What Becomes of the Broken Hearted?	1999	Ian Mune	Alan Duff	Bill Gavin Richard Sheffield (executive)
What Dreams May Come	1998	Vincent Ward	Richard Matheson (novel What Dreams May Come) Ronald Bass (screenplay)	Barnet Bain Ronald Bass (executive) Alan C. Blomquist (co-producer) Stephen Deutsch (as Stephen Simon) Ted Field (executive) Erica Huggins (executive) Scott Kroopf (executive)
When We Were Kings	1996	Leon Gast		Leon Gast Taylor Hackford Vikram Jayanti (co-producer) Keith Robinson (co-producer) David Sonnenberg (executive)
Wild at Heart	1990	David Lynch	Barry Gifford (novel) David Lynch (screenplay)	Steve Golin Michael Kuhn (executive) Monty Montgomery Sigurjon Sighvatsson
Wonderland	1999	Michael Winterbottom	Laurence Coriat	Michelle Camarda (co-producer) Gina Carter (co-producer) Andrew Eaton (co-producer) Anita Overland (line) David M. Thompson (executive) Stewart Till (executive)
Young Americans, The	1993	Danny Cannon	Danny Cannon David Hilton	Richard N. Gladstein (executive) Philippe Maigret (executive) Alison Owen Paul Trijbits Ronna B. Wallace (executive)
Your Friends & Neighbors	1998	Neil LaBute	Neil LaBute (written by)	Steve Golin Alix Madigan (executive) (as Alix Madigan-Yorkin) Jason Patric Stephen Pevner (executive) Philip Steuer (co-producer)

Cinematograhy	Film Editing	Special Effects	Production Design	Costume Design	Cast includes
David Hennings	Dan Lebental	John P. Mesa Dan Novy	Dina Lipton	Terry Dresbach	Jon Favreau Leland Orser Cameron Diaz Christian Slater
Tom Richmond	Jeff Wishengrad	Pierre 'Bill' Rivard	Zoé Sakellaropoulo	Rene April	Billy Crudup Jennifer Connelly Molly Parker Janet McTeer
Allen Guilford	D. Michael Horton		Brett Schwieter	Pauline Bowkett	Julian Arahanga Nancy Brunning Tammy Davis Clint Eruera
Eduardo Serra	David Brenner Maysie Hoy	Wayne Billheimer Andrew Perkins Gerard Benjamin Pierre Talmage Watson	Eugenio Zanetti	Yvonne Blake	Robin Williams Cuba Gooding Jr Annabella Sciorra Max von Sydow
Maryse Alberti Paul Goldsmith Kevin Keating Albert Maysles Roderick Young	Leon Gast Taylor Hackford Jeffrey Levy-Hinte Keith Robinson				Muhammad Ali George Foreman Don King James Brown
Frederick Elmes	Duwayne Dunham	Don Power	Patricia Norris	Amy Stofsky	Nicolas Cage Laura Dern Willem Dafoe J.E. Freeman
Sean Bobbitt	Trevor Waite		Mark Tildesley	Natalie Ward	Shirley Henderson Gina McKee Molly Parker Ian Hart
Vernon Layton	Alex Mackie		Laurence Dorman	Howard Burden	Harvey Keitel Iain Glen John Wood Terence Rigby
Nancy Schreiber	Joel Plotch	David Fiske Ray McIntyre Jr	Charles Breen	Lynette Meyer April Napier	Amy Brenneman Aaron Eckhart Catherine Keener Nastassja Kinski

6
Awards

Adventures of Priscilla, Queen of the Desert (1994)

Academy Award (1995)
- Best Costume Design

Australian Film Institute (1994)
- Best Achievement in Costume Design
- Best Achievement in Production Design
- 6 Nominations

British Academy Awards (1995)
- Best Costume Design
- Best Make-Up/Hair
- 4 Nominations

Gay and Lesbian Alliance Against Defamation Media Awards (1995)
- Outstanding Film

Golden Globes (1995)
- 2 Nominations
- Seattle International Film Festival (1994)
- Best Actor (Terence Stamp)
- Best Film

Writers Guild of America (1995)
- 1 Nomination

American Werewolf in London, An (1981)

Academy Awards (1982)
- Best Make-up

Academy of Science Fiction, Horror and Fantasy Films (1982)
- Best Horror Film

Backbeat (1993)

British Academy Awards (1995)
- Anthony Asquith Award for Film Music

- 2 Nominations

Cleveland International Film Festival (1994)
- Best Film

Ballad of Little Jo, The (1993)

Independent Spirit Awards (1994)
- 2 Nominations

Barb Wire (1996)

MTV Movie Awards
- Best Fight (Pamela Anderson)

Razzie Awards
- Worst New Star (Pamela Anderson)

- 5 Nominations (Worst Actress, Worst Original Song, Worst Picture, Worst Screen Couple, Worst Screenplay)

Barney's Great Adventure (1998)

Razzie Awards
- 2 Nominations (Worst New Star, Worst Original Song)

Barton Fink (1991)

Academy Awards (1992)
- 3 Nominations (Best Art Direction, Best Costume Design, Best Supporting Actor)

Cannes Film Festival (1991)
- Best Actor (John Turturro)
- Best Director (Joel Coen)
- Golden Palm (Joel Coen)

David di Donatello Awards (1992)
- Best Foreign Actor (John Turturro)

Golden Globes
- 1 Nomination (Best Performance by an Actor in a Supporting Role)

Los Angeles Film Critics Association Awards
- Best Cinematography (Roger Deakins)
- Best Supporting Actor (Michael Lerner)

National Society of Film Critics Awards
- Best Cinematography (Roger Deakins)

New York Film Critics Circle Awards
- Best Cinematography (Roger Deakins)
- Best Supporting Actress (Judy Davis)

Bean (1997)

Golden Screen (Germany, 1997)
- Golden Screen

Being John Malkovich (1999)

Academy Awards (2000)
- 3 Nominations (Best Actress in a Supporting Role, Best Director, Best Writing)

Academy of Science Fiction, Horror and Fantasy Films (2000)

- Best Fantasy Film

- Best Writer (Charlie Kaufman)

- 1 Nomination (Best Actress)

American Comedy Awards (2000)

- 3 Nominations

British Academy Awards (2000)

- Best Screenplay (Charlie Kaufman)

- 2 Nominations

César Awards (France, 2000)

- 1 Nomination (Best Foreign Film)

Deauville Film Festival (1999)

- Critics Award (Spike Jonze)

- Grand Special Prize (Spike Jonze)

Directors Guild of America (2000)

- 1 Nomination

Gay and Lesbian Alliance Against Defamation (GLAAD) Media Awards

- Outstanding Film

Golden Globes (2000)

- 3 Nominations

Independent Spirit Awards (2000)

- Best First Feature – Over $500 000

- Best First Screenplay (Charlie Kaufman)

- 1 Nomination

MTV Movie Awards (2000)

- Best New Filmmaker (Spike Jonze)

National Society of Film Critics Awards (2000)

- Best Film (with Topsy-Turvy)

- Best Screenplay Charlie Kaufman)

New York Film Critics Circle Awards (1999)
- Best First Film (Spike Jonze)

- Best Supporting Actor (John Malkovich)

- Best Supporting Actress (Catherine Keener)

Online Film Critics Society Awards (2000)
- Best Debut (Spike Jonze)

- Best Original Screenplay (Charlie Kauffman)

- Best Supporting Actress (Catherine Keener)

- 6 Nominations

The Big Lebowski (1998)

Berlin International Film Festival (1998)
- 1 Nomination

European Film Awards (1998)
- 1 Nomination

Golden Satellite Awards (1998)
- 3 Nominations

Bob Roberts (1992)

Golden Globes (1993)
- 1 Nomination (Best Performance)

Tokyo International Film Festival (1992)
- Bronze Award (Tim Robbins)

Borrowers, The (1997)

British Academy Awards (1998)
- 2 Nominations

Motion Picture Sound Editors (1999)
- Best Sound Editing – Foreign Feature

Bound (1996)

Independent Spirit Awards (1997)
* 1 Nomination (Best Cinematography)

MTV Movie Awards (1997)
* 1 Nomination (Best Kiss)

Stockholm Film Festival (1996)
* Honourable Mention
* 1 Nomination

Candyman (1992)

Avoriaz Fantastic Film Festival (1993)
* 1 Nomination

Fantasporto (Portugal) (1993)
* 1 Nomination

Carrington (1995)

British Academy Awards (1996)
* 2 Nominations

Cannes Film Festival (1995)
* Best Actor (Jonathan Pryce)
* Jury Special Prize (Christopher Hampton)

Stranger Among Us, A aka Close to Eden (1992)

Cannes Film Festival (1992)
* 1 Nomination

Fantasporto (1993)
* 1 Nomination

Razzie Awards (1993)
* Worst Actress (Melanie Griffiths)
* 1 Nomination (Worst Supporting Actress)

Dangerous Woman, A (1993)

Golden Globes (1994)
- 1 Nomination

Tokyo International Film Festival (1994)
- Best Actress (Debra Winger)

Dead Man Walking (1995)

Academy Awards (1995)
- Best Actress (Susan Sarandon)
- 3 Nominations (Best Actor, Best Director, Best Music)

Berlin International Film Festival (1996)
- Prize of the Ecumenical Jury (Tim Robbins)
- Prize of the Guild of German Art House Cinemas (Tim Robbins)
- Reader Jury (Tim Robbins)
- 1 Nomination (Golden Bear)

Independent Spirit Awards (1996)
- Best Male Lead (Sean Pean)
- 1 Nomination

Political Film Society (1997)
- Exposé
- 1 Nomination

Screen Actors Guild Awards (1996)
- Outstanding Female Actor (Susan Sarandon)
- 1 Nomination

Dream Lover (1986)

Avoriaz Fantastic Film Festival (1986)
- Grand Prize

Edward II (1991)

Berlin International Film Festival (1992)
- FIPRESCI award

- Teddy (Best Feature Film)

Venice Film Festival (1991)
- Best Actress (Tilda Swinton)

Elizabeth (1998)

Academy Awards (1999)
- Best Makeup

- 6 Nominations (Best Actress, Best Art Direction, Best Cinematographer, Best Costume Design, Best Music, Best Picture)

British Academy Awards (1999)
- Alexander Korda Award for Best British Film

- Anthony Asquith Award for Film Music

- Best Cinematography

- Best Makeup

- Best Supporting Actor (Geoffrey Rush)

- Best Actress (Cate Blanchett)

- 6 Nominations

Broadcast Film Critics Association Awards (1999)
- Best Actress (Cate Blanchett)

- Breakthrough Artist (Joseph Fiennes)

- 1 Nomination (Best Picture)

Golden Globes (1999)
- Best Actress (Cate Blanchett)

- 2 Nominations

London Film Critics Circle Awards (1999)
- Actress of the Year (Cate Blanchett)

- Best Producer of the Year (Tim Bevan, Eric Fellner, Alison Owen)

Online Film Critics Society Award (1999)

- Best Actress (Cate Blanchett)

Venice Film Festival (1998)

- Max Factor Award (Best Makeup)

Fargo (1996)

Academy Awards (1997)

- Best Actress (Frances McDormand)

- Best Screenplay (Ethan and Joel Coen)

- 5 Nominations (Best Cinematography, Best Director, Best Film Editing, Best Picture, Best Supporting Actor)

American Comedy Awards (1997)

- Funniest Actress (Frances McDormand)

Australian Film Critics Circle Awards (1997)

- Best Foreign Film

Australian Film Institute (1996)

- Best Foreign Film

British Academy Awards (1997)

- David Lean Award for Direction (Joel Coen)

- 5 Nominations

Cannes Film Festival (1996)

- Best Director (Joel Coen)

- 1 Nomination (Golden Palm)

London Film Critics Circle Awards (1997)

- Actress of the Year

- Director of the Year

- Film of the Year

- Screenwriter of the Year

New York Film Critics Circle Awards (1996)

- Best Film

Screen Actors Guild Awards (1997)

* Outstanding Female Performance (Frances McDormand)

* 1 Nomination

Writers Guild of America (1997)

* Best Screenplay (Joel and Ethan Coen)

Four Weddings and a Funeral (1994)

Academy Awards (1995)

* 2 Nominations (Best Picture, Best Writer)

Australian Film Institute (1994)

* Best Foreign Film

British Academy Awards (1995)

* Best Leading Actor (Hugh Grant)

* Best Supporting Actress (Kristin Scott Thomas)

* Best Film

* David Lean Award for Best Direction (Mike Newell)

* 6 Nominations (Anthony Asquith Award for Film Music, Best Supporting Actor, Best Supporting Actress, Best Costume Design, Best Editing, Best Original Screenplay)

César Awards (France, 1995)

* Best Foreign Film

Evening Standard British Film Awards (1995)

* Best Actress (Kristin Scott Thomas)

Golden Globes (1995)

* Best Actor in a Comedy/Musical (Hugh Grant)

* 3 Nominations (Best Motion Picture, Best Actress, Best Screenplay)

Golden Screen (Germany, 1994)

* Golden Screen Award

MTV Movie Awards (1995)

* Best Breakthrough Performance (Hugh Grant)

Writers Guild of America (1995)

* Best Screenplay (Richard Curtis)

The Green Mile (1999)

Academy Awards (2000)
- 4 Nominations (Best Supporting Actor, Best Picture, Best Sound, Best Screenplay)

Academy of Science Fiction, Horror and Fantasy Films (2000)
- Best Action/Adventure/Thriller
- Best Supporting Actor (Michael Clarke Duncan)
- Best Supporting Actress (Patricia Clarkson)
- 2 Nomintions

Blockbuster Entertainment Awards (2000)
- Favorite Actor (Tom Hanks)
- 2 Nominations

Broadcast Film Critics Awards (2000)
- Best Adapted Screenplay (Frank Darabont)
- Best Supporting Actor (Michael Clarke Duncan)
- 1 Nomination (Best Picture)

People's Choice Awards (2001)
- Favorite Dramatic Motion Picture
- Favorite Motion Picture

Political Film Society (2000)
- Human Rights

Haine, La (1995)

Cannes Film Festival (1995)
- Best Director (Mathieu Kassovitz)
- 1 Nomination (Golden Palm)

César Awards (France, 1996)
- Best Editor (Matheiu Kassovitz and Scott Stevenson)
- Best Film
- Best Producer (Christophe Rossignon)
- 6 Nominations

European Film Awards (1995)
- Young European Film of the Year

Home for the Holidays (1995)

Young Artist Awards (1996)
- Best Young Leading Actress (Claire Danes)

Home of Our Own, A (1993)

Young Artist Awards (1993)
- Best Leading Youth Actor (Edward Furlong)
- 3 Nominations

Hudsucker Proxy, The (1994)

Cannes Film Festival (1994)
- 1 Nomination (Golden Palm)

Los Angeles Film Critics Association Awards (1994)
- Best Production Design (Dennis Gassner)

Huitième jour, Le (1996)

Cannes Film Festival (1996)
- Best Actor (Daniel Auteuil and Pascal Duquenne)
- 1 Nomination (Golden Palm)

Flanders International Film Festival (1996)
- Best Belgian Actor (Pascal Duquenne)
- Best Belgian Director (Jaco van Dormael)
- Best Belgian Film
- Joseph Plateau Box Office Award

Jude (1996)

Evening Standard British Film Awards (1996)
- Best Actress (Kate Winslett)

Jumanji (1995)

Academy of Science Fiction, Horror and Fantasy Films (1995)
- Best Actress (Bonnie Hunt)

Young Artist Awards (1996)
- Best Family Feature – Action/Adventure
- 1 Nomination

Kalifornia (1993)

Montréal World Film Festival (1993)
- Best Artistic Contribution (Dominic Sena)

Kill Me Again (1989)

Cognac Festival du Film Policier (1990)
- Grand Prix (John Dahl)

Life Less Ordinary, A (1997)

MTV Movie Awards (1998)
- 2 Nominations

Lock, Stock and Two Smoking Barrels (1998)

British Academy Awards (1999)
- Audience Award
- 2 Nominations (Best British Film, Best Editing)

Evening Standard British Film Awards (1999)
- Most Promising Newcomer (Guy Ritchie)

London Film Critics Circle Awards (1999)
- British Film of the Year
- British Screenwriter of the Year (Guy Ritchie)

MTV Movie Awards (1999)

- Best New Filmmaker (Guy Ritchie)

Tokyo International Film Festival (1998)

- Best Director (Guy Ritchie)

Map of the Human Heart (1992)

Australian Film Institute (1993)

- Young Actors Awards (Robert Joamie)

- 6 Nominations

Tokyo International Film Festival (1993)

- Best Artistic Contribution (Vincent Ward)

Mr. Holland's Opus (1995)

Academy Awards (1996)

- 1 Nomination (Best Actor – Richard Dreyfuss)

Golden Globes (1996)

- 2 Nominations

Young Artist Awards (1996)

- Best Family Feature: Drama

- Best Performance by Under 10 (Nicholas John Renner)

- 1 Nomination

Nell (1994)

Academy Awards (1994)

- 1 Nomination (Best Actress: Jodie Foster)

Screen Actors Guild Awards (1995)

- Outstanding Performance by a Female Actor (Jodie Foster)

Notting Hill (1999)

Blockbuster Entertainment Awards (2000)
- 4 Nominations

Brit Awards (2000)
- Best Soundtrack

British Academy Awards (2000)
- Audience Award
- 2 Nominations (Best Film, Best Supporting Actor)

European Film Awards (1999)
- 1 Nomination (Best Film)

Evening Standard British Film Awards (2000)
- Peter Sellers Award for Comedy (John de Borman)

Golden Globes (2000)
- 3 Nominations

Golden Screen (Germany, 1999)
- Golden Screen

Nurse Betty (2000)

Cannes Film Festival (2000)
- Best Screenplay
- 1 Nomination (Golden Palm)

Golden Globes (2001)
- Best Actress (Renée Zellwegger)

Photographing Fairies (1997)

Fantafestival (Italy, 1998)
- Grand Prize of European Fantasy Film

Fantasporto (Portugal, 1998)
- Grand Prize (Silver)
- Best Special Effects
- 1 Nomination (International Fantasy Film Award)

Portrait of a Lady, The (1996)

Academy Awards (1997)
- 2 Nominations (Best Costume Design, Best Supporting Actress: Barbara Hershey)

Golden Globes (1997)
- 1 Nomination (Best Supporting Actress)

Los Angeles Film Critics Association Awards (1996)
- Best Production Design (Janet Patterson)
- Best Supporting Actress (Barbara Hershey)

National Society of Film Critics Awards (1997)
- Best Supporting Actor (Martin Donovan)
- Best Supporting Actress (Barbara Hershey)

Red Rock West (1992)

Independent Spirit Awards (1995)
- 2 Nominations (Best Director, Best Screenplay)

Ridicule (1996)

Academy Awards (1997)
- 1 Nomination (Best Foreign Language Film)

British Academy Awards (1997)
- Best Film not in the English Language

Cannes Film Festival (1996)
- 1 Nomination (Golden Palm)

César Awards (France, 1997)
- Best Costume Design
- Best Director (Patrice Leconte)
- Best Film
- Best Production Design
- 6 Nominations

Golden Globes (1997)
- 1 Nomination (Best Foreign Language Film)

Savage Nights/Les Nuits Fauves (1992)

César Awards (France, 1993)
- Best Editor (Lisa Beaulieu)
- Best Film
- Best New Director (Cyril Collard)
- Most Promising Young Actress (Romane Bohringer)
- 3 Nominations

Shallow Grave (1994)

British Academy Awards (1995)
- Alexander Korda Award for Best British Film

Cognac Festival du Film Policier (1995)
- Audience Award
- Grand Prix

Fantasporto (Portugal, 1995)
- International Fantasy Film Award

London Film Critics Circle Awards (1996)
- Best Newcomer of the Year (Danny Boyle)

Sleepers (1996)

Academy Awards (1997)
- 1 Nomination (Best Music)

Snow White (1997)

American Society of Cinematographers (1998)
- 1 Nomination (Outstanding Achievement in Cinematography)

Emmy Awards (1998)
- 3 Nominations (Costume Design, Lead Actress, Makeup)

Screen Actors Guild Awards (1998)
- 1 Nomination (Best Female Actor: Sigourney Weaver)

Spice World (1997)

Blockbuster Entertainment Awards (1999)
* 1 Nomination (Best Actress: Victoria Beckham, Melanie Brown, Emma Bunton, Melanie Chisholm, Geri Halliwell)

Razzie Awards (1999)
* Worst Actress (Victoria Beckham, Melanie Brown, Emma Bunton, Melanie Chisholm, Geri Halliwell)
* 6 Nominations (Worst New Star, Worst Original Song, Worst Picture, Worst Screen Couple, Worst Screenplay, Worst Supporting Actor)

Thousand Acres, A (1997)

Golden Globes (1998)
* 1 Nomination (Best Actress: Jessica Lange)

Verona Love Screens Festival (1999)
* Best Actress (Jessica Lange, Jennifer Jason-Leigh and Michelle Pfeiffer)

Trainspotting (1996)

Academy Awards (1997)
* 1 Nomination (Best Screenplay)

Boston Society of Film Critics Awards (1996)
* Best Film

Brit Awards (1997)
* Best Soundtrack

British Academy Awards (1996)
* Best Screenplay (John Hodge)
* 1 Nomination (Best Film)

Evening Standard British Film Awards (1997)
* Best Screenplay (John Hodge)

London Film Critics Circle Awards (1997)

- British Actor of the Year (Ewan McGregor)
- British Screenwriter of the Year (John Hodge)
- 2 Nominations (Director and Film of the Year)

Seattle International Film Festival (1996)

- Best Director (Danny Boyle)
- Best Film

Un coeur en hiver (1992)

British Academy Awards (1994)

- 1 Nomination (Best Film not in the English Language)

César Awards (France, 1993)

- Best Director (Claude Sautet)
- Best Supporting Actor (André Dussollier)
- 7 Nominations

European Film Awards (1993)

- Best Actor (Daniel Auteuil)

Venice Film Festival (1992)

- FIPRESCI Award (Claude Sautet)
- Silver Lion (Claude Sautet)

Usual Suspects, The (1995)

Academy Awards (1996)

- Best Supporting Actor (Kevin Spacey)
- Best Screenplay (Christopher McQuarrie)

Academy of Science Fiction, Horror and Fantasy Films (1995)

- Best Musical Score

Boston Society of Film Critics Awards (1995)

- Best Supporting Actor (Kevin Spacey)

British Academy Awards (1996)

- Best Editing (John Ottman)

- Best Film

- Best Screenplay (Christopher McQuarrie)

Chicago Film Critics Association Awards (1996)

- Best Screenplay (Christopher McQuarrie)

- Best Supporting Actor (Kevin Spacey)

Independent Spirit Awards (1996)

- Best Screenplay (Christopher McQuarrie)

- Best Supporting Male (Benicio del Toro)

- 1 Nomination (Best Cinematography)

New York Film Critics Circle Awards (1995)

- Best Supporting Actor (Kevin Spacey)

Seattle International Film Festival (1995)

- Best Actor (Kevin Spacey)

- Best Director (Bryan Singer)

Tokyo International Film Festival (1995)

- Silver Award (Bryan Singer)

What Dreams May Come (1998)

Academy Awards (1999)

- Best Effects, Visual Effects

- 1 Nomination (Best Art Direction)

Blockbuster Entertainment Awards (1999)

- Favorite Supporting Actor (Cuba Gooding Jr.)

International Monitor Awards (1999)

- Electronic Visual Effects

Society of Motion Picture and Television Art Directors (1999)

- Award for Excellence in Production Design

When We Were Kings (1996)

Academy Awards (1997)
- Best Documentary Feature

Sundance Film Festival (1996)
- Special Recognition (Leon Gast – director)

Wild at Heart (1990)

Academy Awards (1991)
- 1 Nomination (Best Supporting Actress: Diane Ladd)

British Academy Awards (1991)
- 1 Nomination (Best Sound)

Cannes Film Festival (1990)
- Golden Palm (David Lynch)

Independent Spirit Awards (1991)
- Best Cinematography (Frederick Elmes)
- 1 Nomination (Best Supporting Male: Willem Dafoe)

Wonderland (1999)

British Academy Awards (2000)
- 1 Nomination (Best British Film)

British Independent Film Awards (1999)
- Best British Film
- 2 Nominations (Best Actress, Best Director)

Cannes Film Festival (1999)
- 1 Nomination (Golden Palm)

7
PolyGram Companies

Production/management

- A&M USA
- Casablanca FilmWorks (1976-1979)
- Cinea (France: 50%)
- Hong Kong Ted Poly (50%)
- Interscope Communications
- MFP/Meteor (Benelux: Jan 94)
- Midi Minuit (France: 50%)
- Noe Productions (France: 50%)
- PolyGram Film Productions (Netherlands)
- PolyGram Filmed Entertainment (UK)
- PolyGram Filmed Entertainment (US)
- PolyGram Filmproduktions (Germany)
- PolyGram Films (UK)
- PolyGram Music Video International
- PolyGram Pictures (1980-1982)
- Propaganda
- R Films (France: 50%)
- Really Useful Holdings (Andrew Lloyd Webber, UK: 30%)
- Working Title Films

Distribution

- Gramercy (US)
- Manifesto Film Sales
- MFP/Meteor (Benelux)
- Pan Europeanne (France)
- PFE Australia
- PFE Germany
- PFE Italy
- PFE Switzerland
- PolyGram Film International
- PolyGram Films (US)
- Sogepaq (Spain)

Output deals

- Act III
- David Fincher
- Def. Pictures (Russell Simmons)
- Dirty Hands Production (Alan Parker)
- Egg Pictures (Jodie Foster)
- Havoc Inc. (Tim Robbins)
- Ivan Reitman / Tom Pollock
- Jason Patric
- Revolution Films
- Specific Films

Other

- WTTV Ltd.

8
Corporate structure – PolyGram Filmed Entertainment

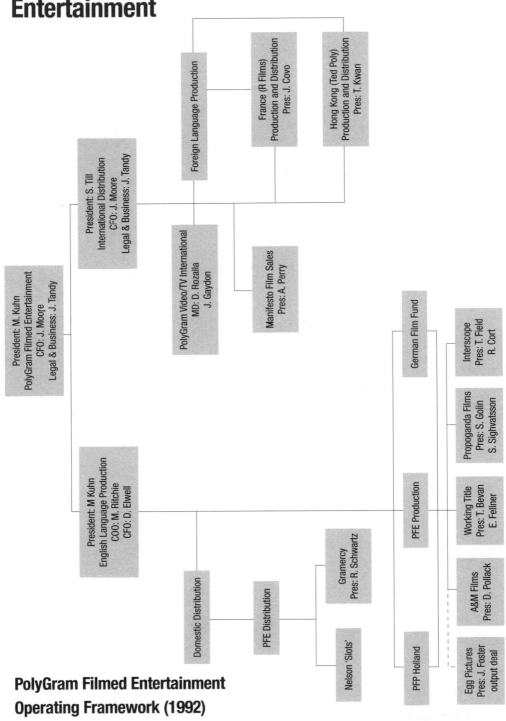

PolyGram Filmed Entertainment
Operating Framework (1992)

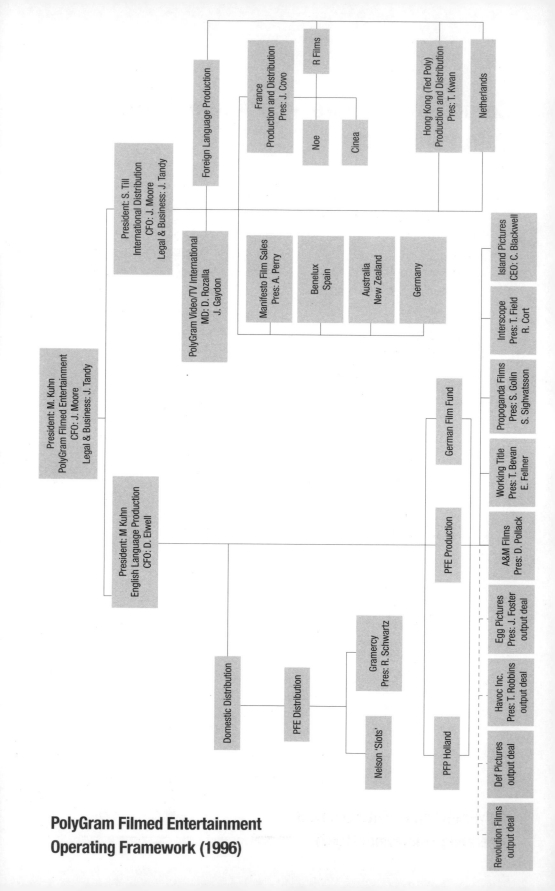

**PolyGram Filmed Entertainment
Operating Framework (1996)**

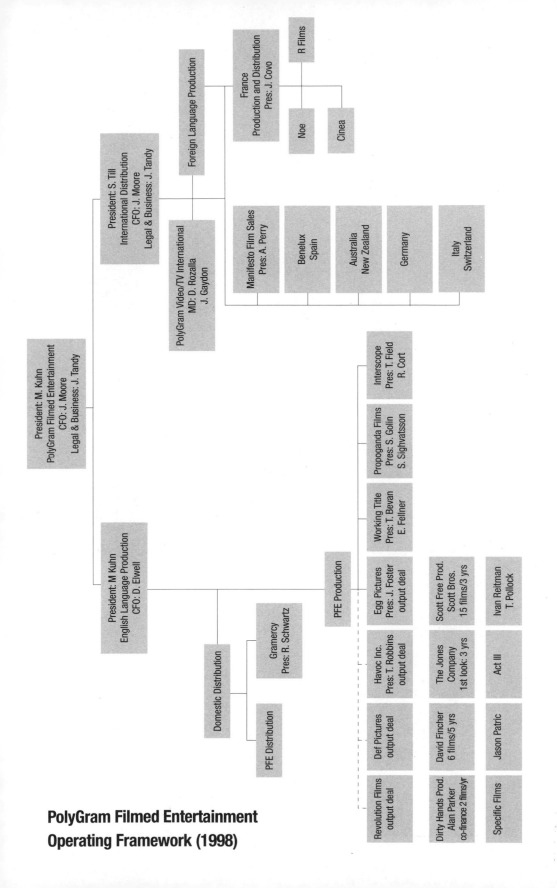

**PolyGram Filmed Entertainment
Operating Framework (1998)**

PolyGram Filmed Entertainment
Balance of Power

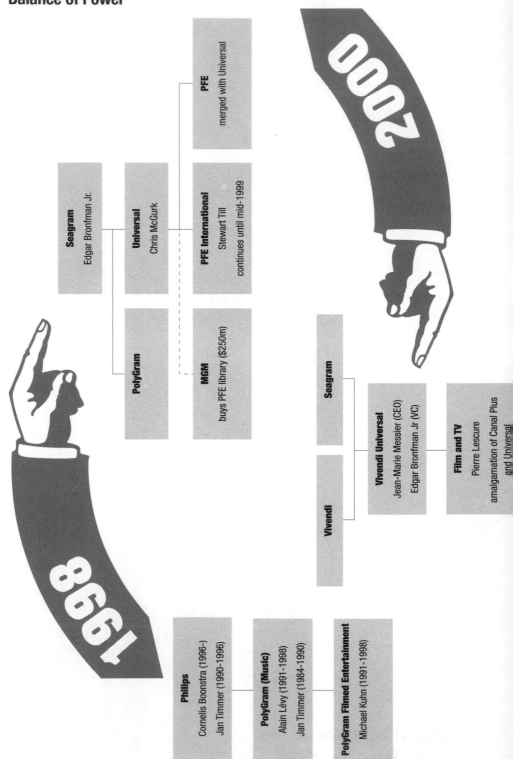

1998

Philips
Cornelis Boonstra (1996–)
Jan Timmer (1990–1996)

PolyGram (Music)
Alain Lévy (1991–1998)
Jan Timmer (1984–1990)

PolyGram Filmed Entertainment
Michael Kuhn (1991–1998)

Seagram
Edgar Bronfman Jr.

Universal
Chris McGurk

PolyGram

PFE International
Stewart Till
continues until mid-1999

PFE
merged with Universal

MGM
buys PFE library ($250m)

Seagram

Vivendi

Vivendi Universal
Jean-Marie Messier (CEO)
Edgar Bronfman Jr (VC)

Film and TV
Pierre Lescure
amalgamation of Canal Plus
and Universal

2000

9
Index

Film, song and book titles are in italics.

C

D

E

R

S